A Common Core Approach To Teaching

THE GREAT GATSBY

Literature Lesson Plans

Written To The Common Core Standards

Teacher's Pet Publications

ISBN 978-1-60249-502-9

Teacher's Pet Publications
11504 Hammock Point Road
Berlin, Maryland 21811
www.tpet.com

Table Of Contents

Table Of Contents, Continued

MATERIALS: CHAPTERS 1-2

THE GREAT GATSBY

Reading Activity 1: True or False

Reading Activity 2: Analyzing Passages

Reading Activity 3: Physical Attributes & Characterization

Reading Activity 4: Action, Character, Decision

Reading Activity 5: Figurative Language

Reading Activity 6: Elements of Fiction & Literary Devices

Reading Activity 7: Meaning and Inferences

Writing Activity 1: How Do Men Relate To One Another

Suggested Writing Assignments

Quick-Write Assignments

NOTES
THE GREAT GATSBY

The Great Gatsby Chapters 1-2

Reading Activity 1: True or False?

Anchor Standard	11th-12th Grade
CCRA.R.1	RL.11-12.1
CCRA.SL1	SL.11-12.1
CCRA SL.4	SL.11-12.4

Objectives

- Students will be able to cite the parts of the text that support their analysis of what the text says or infers.
- Students will consider statements about the text, determine whether those statements are true or false, and will give textual evidence supporting their choices.
- Students will work together in small groups to discuss, analyze, and evaluate the statements made.
- Students will evaluate the analytical work of their peers.

Directions

Prior to reading chapters 1-2: Give students (or post) the following list of statements about the chapters, and explain to students that they should read chapters 1-2 to find out if these statements are true or false:

Daisy is aware that Tom is having an extramarital affair.
Daisy will not divorce Tom because she is Catholic.
Nick believes that it is acceptable to look down on the working class.
Tom treats George with respect.
Myrtle is an elegant and sophisticated woman.
Nick leaves the party and goes directly home.

After reading chapters 1-2: The worksheets on the following pages can be done by students individually, in small groups, or as a whole class. Below are directions to use the questions as a group activity to fulfill more state standards:

- Cut the worksheet apart, making each question and answer box a slip.
- Divide your class into six groups and give one question and a True/False evaluation form to each group. Tell students they are to discuss the statement and determine if the statement is true or false, supporting their decision with evidence from the text. Tell them their answers will be evaluated on the criteria given on the evaluation form.
- Give students ample time to discuss the statements and record their answers.
- Have the groups swap True or False question slips so that each group can evaluate another group's answer. The group should fill in the number of the question they are evaluating, decide how well the answer fulfills the criteria listed, and fill out the form accordingly.
- Repeat the previous step until all the groups have evaluated each others' answers.
- Collect the evaluations and answer slips.

The Great Gatsby Chapters 1-2: True or False?

Write *True* or *False* in the blank next to each statement. Below the statement, explain why you chose true or false, referencing the text to support your choices.

__________ 1. Daisy is aware that Tom is having an extramarital affair.

__________ 2. Daisy will not divorce Tom because she is Catholic.

__________ 3. Nick believes that it is acceptable to look down on the working class.

__________ 4. Tom treats George with respect.

__________ 5. Myrtle is an elegant and sophisticated woman.

__________ 6. Nick leaves the party and goes directly home.

The Great Gatsby Chapters 1-2 True or False? Evaluation

List Your Group's Members: Your Group's Question # _______

___________________ ___________________ ___________________

___________________ ___________________ ___________________

1 = No, Not At All **2** = A Little **3** = Some **4** = Yes **5** = Yes, Very Well

Evaluation of Question # ___

Does the explanation support the answer of true or false? 1 2 3 4 5
Is there good textual evidence to support the answer? 1 2 3 4 5
Is the answer clearly stated? 1 2 3 4 5
Total Score ________ of a possible 15 points

Evaluation of Question # ___

Does the explanation support the answer of true or false? 1 2 3 4 5
Is there good textual evidence to support the answer? 1 2 3 4 5
Is the answer clearly stated? 1 2 3 4 5
Total Score ________ of a possible 15 points

Evaluation of Question # ___

Does the explanation support the answer of true or false? 1 2 3 4 5
Is there good textual evidence to support the answer? 1 2 3 4 5
Is the answer clearly stated? 1 2 3 4 5
Total Score ________ of a possible 15 points

Evaluation of Question # ___

Does the explanation support the answer of true or false? 1 2 3 4 5
Is there good textual evidence to support the answer? 1 2 3 4 5
Is the answer clearly stated? 1 2 3 4 5
Total Score ________ of a possible 15 points

Evaluation of Question # ___

Does the explanation support the answer of true or false? 1 2 3 4 5
Is there good textual evidence to support the answer? 1 2 3 4 5
Is the answer clearly stated? 1 2 3 4 5
Total Score ________ of a possible 15 points

The Great Gatsby Chapters 1-2: True or False? Suggested Answers

Write *True* or *False* in the blank next to each statement. Below the statement, explain why you chose true or false, referencing the text to support your choices.

True 1. Daisy is aware that Tom is having an extramarital affair.

> Daisy exits the room, prompted by the call to Tom. Jordan interrupts Nick so she can eavesdrop on the exchange between Daisy and Tom. Jordan intimates that everyone—conceivably also Daisy—knows that Tom "has a woman in New York," or that he is carrying on an extramarital affair.

False 2. Daisy will not divorce Tom because she is Catholic.

> Catherine tells this to Nick at the get-together at Tom's love nest in the city: "'You see,' cried Catherine triumphantly. She lowered her voice again. 'It's really his wife that's keeping them apart. She's a Catholic, and they don't believe in divorce.'" Nick follows up this information with narration to the reader: "Daisy was not a Catholic, and I was a little shocked at the elaborateness of the lie."

False 3. Nick believes that it is acceptable to look down on the working class.

> Nick identifies himself as different from those in his well-to-do family and says that he "reserves judgment." Nick tries to remember that he is more fortunate than others: "I am still a little afraid of missing something if I forget that, as my father snobbishly suggested, and I snobbishly repeat, a sense of the fundamental decencies is parceled out unequally at birth."

False 4. Tom treats George with respect.

> Tom is openly patronizing and rude to George, who he sees as many social levels beneath him. The car deal that he talks to George about is not particularly serious; rather, it is a ruse for Tom to interact with Myrtle and humiliate George. Tom remarks about George, "He's so dumb he doesn't know he's alive."

False 5. Myrtle is an elegant and sophisticated woman.

Myrtle is not, though she may believe that her association with Tom elevates her social standing. Behaviors like purchasing gossip magazines and commenting on how poor the service is show her to lack social graces and to be somewhat vulgar. Even the way she has decorated the apartment with garish and oversized furniture speaks to this quality of being a poseur or wannabe inherent in Myrtle.

True 6. Nick leaves the party and goes directly home.

Nick goes to Mr. McKee's apartment and looks at his photographs, in what seems like an intimate encounter. He catches the train at 4 a.m.

The Great Gatsby Chapters 1-2

Reading Activity 2: Analyzing Passages

Anchor Standard	11th-12th Grade
CCRA.R.6	RL.11-12.1
	RL.11-12.4
CCRA.SL.1	SL.11-12.1

Objectives

- Students will cite strong and thorough textual evidence to support analysis of what the text says explicitly as well as inferences drawn from the text, including determining where the text leaves matters uncertain.
- Determine the meaning of words and phrases as they are used in the text, including figurative and connotative meanings; analyze the impact of specific word choices on meaning and tone, including words with multiple meanings or language that is particularly fresh, engaging, or beautiful.
- Analyze a case in which grasping a point of view requires distinguishing what is directly stated in a text from what is really meant (e.g., satire, sarcasm, irony, or understatement). Students will analyze the impact of specific word choices on meaning and tone.

Directions

On the pages that follow, there are 8 passages to analyze, each with a question or questions to guide the process. There are many ways to use these questions:

- You could use them as a worksheet for all students to complete individually.
- You could use the worksheet as your guide in a whole-class discussion. Have students turn to the first passage in the book, read it, and then ask the question(s) orally. Repeat through all 8 questions.
- You could assign one passage to each of 8 different groups of students, for the students to discuss and come up with responses to the question(s). Then hold a whole-class discussion.
- You could read the passage and then see which student can find the passage first (to practice skimming skills). Then follow up with the questions(s) and discussion.
- You could have students choose one or two questions to respond to in writing in their notebooks or journals.

Follow-Up/Assessment/Extension

- Ask students to gather passages that reveal information about the Buchanan's marriage. Are repetitions or patterns occurring in the passages? What does this indicate about the state of their marriage?

- Have students write about the tension in the scene at Tom and Myrtle's apartment. What caused it?

- Have students pick out other passages in this chapter that show interesting word usage, descriptions, or lack of clarity.

- As an introduction to this activity and these chapters, ask students to write about being part of other people's secrets or poor decisions as a bystander and somewhat unwilling participant, as Nick is in the apartment scene. How has Nick been implicated in Tom's lying?

The Great Gatsby Chapters 1-2 Analyzing Passages

Answer the questions following the quotations completely.

1. "Only Gatsby, the man who gives his name to this book, was exempt from my reaction — Gatsby, who represented everything for which I have an unaffected scorn. If personality is an unbroken series of successful gestures, then there was something gorgeous about him, some heightened sensitivity to the promises of life, as if he were related to one of those intricate machines that register earthquakes ten thousand miles away."

   What does the reference to the book suggest?

2. "When I came back from the East last autumn I felt that I wanted the world to be in uniform and at a sort of moral attention forever; I wanted no more riotous excursions with privileged glimpses into the human heart."

   What words are in conflict within the passage? What does this—and what the speaker yearns for—suggest about the speaker?

3. "But I didn't call to him, for he gave a sudden intimation that he was content to be alone — he stretched out his arms toward the dark water in a curious way, and, far as I was from him, I could have sworn he was trembling. Involuntarily I glanced seaward — and distinguished nothing except a single green light, minute and far away, that might have been the end of a dock. When I looked once more for Gatsby he had vanished, and I was alone again in the unquiet darkness."

   The word "alone" is repeated here; why is that significant?

4. "Miss Baker and I exchanged a short glance consciously devoid of meaning. I was about to speak when she sat up alertly and said 'Sh!' in a warning voice. A subdued impassioned murmur was audible in the room beyond, and Miss Baker leaned forward unashamed, trying to hear. The murmur trembled on the verge of coherence, sank down, mounted excitedly, and then ceased altogether."

   Instead of the words that Daisy is saying, the narrator instead describes the sound with words like "murmur," "tremble," "verge," "sank," and "ceased." What does this indicate about the conversation? About Daisy?

5. "Well, she was less than an hour old and Tom was God knows where. I woke up out of the ether with an utterly abandoned feeling, and asked the nurse right away if it was a boy or a girl. She told me it was a girl, and so I turned my head away and wept. 'All right,' I said, 'I'm glad it's a girl. And I hope she'll be a fool — that's the best thing a girl can be in this world, a beautiful little fool."

   What does Daisy mean by "fool?" How does that relate to the first part of the passage?

6. "Mrs. Wilson had changed her costume some time before, and was now attired in an elaborate afternoon dress of cream-colored chiffon, which gave out a continual rustle as she swept about the room. With the influence of the dress her personality had also undergone a change. The intense vitality that had been so remarkable in the garage was converted into impressive hauteur. Her laughter, her gestures, her assertions became more violently affected moment by moment, and as she expanded the room grew smaller around her, until she seemed to be revolving on a noisy, creaking pivot through the smoky air."

   How does the narrator's view of Myrtle change?

7. "'I told that boy about the ice.'" Myrtle raised her eyebrows in despair at the shiftlessness of the lower orders. 'These people! You have to keep after them all the time.'"

   Why is this ironic? What does it reveal about Myrtle?

8. "The only *crazy* I was was when I married him. I knew right away I made a mistake. He borrowed somebody's best suit to get married in, and never even told me about it, and the man came after it one day when he was out. 'Oh, is that your suit?' I said. 'This is the first I ever heard about it.' But I gave it to him and then I lay down and cried to beat the band all afternoon."

   What is Myrtle suggesting about the basis for her marriage? How might it relate to her willingness to have an affair?

The Great Gatsby Chapters 1-2 Analyzing Passages Suggested Answers

Answer the questions following the quotations completely.

1. "Only Gatsby, the man who gives his name to this book, was exempt from my reaction — Gatsby, who represented everything for which I have an unaffected scorn. If personality is an unbroken series of successful gestures, then there was something gorgeous about him, some heightened sensitivity to the promises of life, as if he were related to one of those intricate machines that register earthquakes ten thousand miles away." What does the reference to the book suggest?

   It suggests that Nick wrote a book about Gatsby. It makes Nick the narrator, but it adds a layer of self-consciousness in perspective; this is the story of Gatsby that Nick presents to the world, which may be different than the way it occurred or the way Nick perceived it while it was actually happening.

2. "When I came back from the East last autumn I felt that I wanted the world to be in uniform and at a sort of moral attention forever; I wanted no more riotous excursions with privileged glimpses into the human heart." What words are in conflict within the passage? What does this—and what the speaker yearns for—suggest about their speaker?

   Words like "uniform" and "attention" are in conflict with the word "riotous." The word "moral" seems to be at odds with "glimpses into the human heart." These conflicts show that the speaker (Nick) wants the world to be an ordered and predictable experience, except it is not. Instead, it is "riotous," volatile, and not able to be controlled. It suggests that Nick is weary of this unpredictable nature of life.

3. "But I didn't call to him, for he gave a sudden intimation that he was content to be alone — he stretched out his arms toward the dark water in a curious way, and, far as I was from him, I could have sworn he was trembling. Involuntarily I glanced seaward — and distinguished nothing except a single green light, minute and far away, that might have been the end of a dock. When I looked once more for Gatsby he had vanished, and I was alone again in the unquiet darkness." The word "alone" is repeated here; why is that significant?

   The word is used to describe both Gatsby and Nick, which unites them and suggests that they are somehow outsiders from privileged society. The first use is somewhat ironic because Gatsby is actually not alone, as Nick is watching him. The use of the word juxtaposed with Gatsby's actions (reaching out in a hug-like way) and the setting ("unquiet darkness") suggests that neither is actually alone.

4. "Miss Baker and I exchanged a short glance consciously devoid of meaning. I was about to speak when she sat up alertly and said 'Sh!' in a warning voice. A subdued impassioned murmur was audible in the room beyond, and Miss Baker leaned forward unashamed, trying to hear. The murmur trembled on the verge of coherence, sank down, mounted excitedly, and then ceased altogether." Instead of the words that Daisy is saying, the narrator instead describes the sound with words like "murmur," "tremble," "verge," "sank," and "ceased." What does this indicate about the conversation? About Daisy?

   What is said is not consequential here, but that the conversation occurs. From Jordan's response, this type of conversation between Daisy and Tom is frequent. Daisy voices her displeasure to Tom over the interruption of his mistress calling their home. The cycle of Daisy's "murmur" shows that she is silenced. Her words have no effect on Tom, and this is even reflected in the withholding of the words from the reader—her complaints are merely a "murmur."

5. "Well, she was less than an hour old and Tom was God knows where. I woke up out of the ether with an utterly abandoned feeling, and asked the nurse right away if it was a boy or a girl. She told me it was a girl, and so I turned my head away and wept. 'All right,' I said, 'I'm glad it's a girl. And I hope she'll be a fool — that's the best thing a girl can be in this world, a beautiful little fool." What does Daisy mean by "fool?" How does that relate to the first part of the passage?

   The first sentence accomplishes something interesting in that it says something but does not say it at all: "Tom was God knows where." While the sentence does not say where Tom was in a direct or forthcoming way, the intimation is that he was involved in an extramarital affair. The word "fool," literally means someone who is fooled or believes something misleading. Daisy's wish for her daughter is to be someone who can be misled. Daisy tries to be a "fool" but cannot, as she is perceptive enough to know Tom is having an affair but wishes she did not know, wishes she could be fooled by his excuses and ignorant of the evidence.

6. "Mrs. Wilson had changed her costume some time before, and was now attired in an elaborate afternoon dress of cream-colored chiffon, which gave out a continual rustle as she swept about the room. With the influence of the dress her personality had also undergone a change. The intense vitality that had been so remarkable in the garage was converted into impressive hauteur. Her laughter, her gestures, her assertions became more violently affected moment by moment, and as she expanded the room grew smaller around her, until she seemed to be revolving on a noisy, creaking pivot through the smoky air." How does the narrator's view of Myrtle change?

   Nick literally describes Myrtle as becoming full of herself, so "affected" that the persona she assumes to be completely subsumes the person she actually is, wife to a gas station proprietor. The progression is negative, even though Nick maintains that he tries to reserve judging others.

7. "'I told that boy about the ice.'" Myrtle raised her eyebrows in despair at the shiftlessness of the lower orders. 'These people! You have to keep after them all the time.'" Why is this ironic? What does it reveal about Myrtle?

   Myrtle herself is in the service profession—the gas station business. Her attitude toward the bell boy differentiates her from working class people ("these people"). Because, unlike Daisy or Tom, Myrtle will never have the prerogatives that position or true social standing provide, her "social mobility" is achieved by putting others down.

8. "The only *crazy* I was was when I married him. I knew right away I made a mistake. He borrowed somebody's best suit to get married in, and never even told me about it, and the man came after it one day when he was out. 'Oh, is that your suit?' I said. 'This is the first I ever heard about it.' But I gave it to him and then I lay down and cried to beat the band all afternoon." What is Myrtle suggesting about the basis for her marriage? How might it relate to her willingness to have an affair?

   She is suggesting that her husband misrepresented himself to be of a higher social standing than he was. Myrtle does not see herself as someone who should be living the life she does—a hardscrabble existence as a gas station operator's wife among the desolate ash heaps. She sees herself as above this, and the role of Tom's mistress as more in line with the person she believes she actually is. This is ironic, however.

The Great Gatsby Chapters 1-2

Reading Activity 3: Physical Attributes and Characterization

Anchor Standard	11th-12th Grade
CCRA.R.1	RL.11-12.1
CCRA.SL.1	SL.11-12.1

Objectives

Using textual evidence, students will explore how physical attributes create meaningful characterization.

Directions

The Physical Attributes and Characterization worksheet on the following page could be used in many ways, completed by small groups of students, individual students, or as a whole class activity.

Students will be able to identify how details describing the physical attributes of characters inform their characterization. Students will observe the way Fitzgerald presents details about characters' physical attributes, including body, mannerisms, gestures, and clothing. Students can revisit this assignment later in the unit to further investigate how the physical descriptions foreshadow plot events in the novel.

Students will concentrate on 3 of 5 potential characters. This allows students to develop expertise in characters of greatest interest to them, or for teachers to assign specific characters to students for more meaningful investigation. Students may (and should) use their books to skim through the chapters to refresh their memories or gather more information about the characters.

After students complete the worksheets discuss students' answers as a whole class. Collect the worksheets for grading, if you choose, or have students put them in their notebooks for further study.

Follow-Up/Assessment/Extension

Revisit this assignment later in the unit and discuss the relationship between characters' physical descriptions and their morality. Is there a correlation? What is it?

The Great Gatsby Chapters 1-2
Reading Activity 3 Physical Attributes and Characterization

From the list of characters below, select three. Locate details about these characters' physical appearance in chapters 1 and 2. Complete the chart below using this evidence from the text. Then, after reviewing the quotes you selected, write about how these physical attributes form a clearer characterization. Use your books to locate significant details about each character's physical appearance (body, mannerisms, gestures, clothing, etc.).

Daisy | Jordan | Tom | George | Myrtle

Character	Quote 1	Quote 2	Quote 3	How do quotes inform characterization?

The Great Gatsby Chapters 1-2
Reading Activity 3 Physical Attributes and Characterization
Suggested Answers

From the list of characters below, select three. Locate details about these characters' physical appearance in chapters 1 and 2. Complete the chart below using this evidence from the text. Then, after reviewing the quotes you selected, write about how these physical attributes form a clearer characterization. Use your books to locate significant details about each character's physical appearance (body, mannerisms, gestures, clothing, etc.).

Daisy | Jordan | Tom | George | Myrtle

Character	Quote 1	Quote 2	Quote 3	How do quotes inform characterization?
Daisy	"I've heard it said that Daisy's murmur was only to make people lean toward her; an irrelevant criticism that made it no less charming."	"I looked back at my cousin, who began to ask me questions in her low, thrilling voice. It was the kind of voice that the ear follows up and down, as if each speech is an arrangement of notes that will never be played again."	"Her face was sad and lovely with bright things in it, bright eyes and a bright passionate mouth, but there was an excitement in her voice that men who had cared for her found difficult to forget: a singing compulsion, a whispered "Listen," a promise that she had done gay, exciting things just a while since and that there were gay, exciting things hovering in the next hour."	Emphasis is on her voice. It enchants men, yet it is not powerful in advocating for herself. Not much emphasis on her body. There is a contradiction in how she looks: "sad" and "lovely."
Jordan	"She was extended full length at her end of the divan, completely motionless, and with her chin raised a little, as if she were balancing something on it which was quite likely to fall."	"Miss Baker's lips fluttered, she nodded at me almost imperceptibly, and then quickly tipped her head back again — the object she was balancing had obviously tottered a little and given her something of a fright."	"She was a slender, small-breasted girl, with an erect carriage, which she accentuated by throwing her body backward at the shoulders like a young cadet. Her gray sun-strained eyes looked back at me with polite reciprocal curiosity out of a wan, charming, discontented face."	The metaphor of balancing something on her chin makes her seem preoccupied or more aware or careful than the others in the room. She is described literally using masculine terms. Not a girly-girl or flirt the way Daisy is.
Tom	"one of the most powerful ends that ever played football at New Haven"	"Now he was a sturdy straw-haired man of thirty with a rather hard mouth and a supercilious manner. Two shining arrogant eyes had established dominance over his face and gave him the appearance of always leaning aggressively forward. Not even the effeminate swank of his riding	"His speaking voice, a gruff husky tenor, added to the impression of fractiousness he conveyed. There was a touch of paternal contempt in it, even toward people he liked — and there were men at New Haven who had hated his guts."	Tom is thoroughly masculine, almost hyper-masculine—"arrogant," "dominance," and "aggressive," are apt descriptors. He is defined almost completely by his body, which is "cruel."

		clothes could hide the enormous power of that body — he seemed to fill those glistening boots until he strained the top lacing, and you could see a great pack of muscle shifting when his shoulder moved under his thin coat. It was a body capable of enormous leverage — a cruel body."		
George	"He was a blond, spiritless man, anaemic, and faintly handsome. When he saw us a damp gleam of hope sprang into his light blue eyes."	"mingling immediately with the cement color of the walls"	"white ashen dust veiled his dark suit and his pale hair as it veiled everything in the vicinity"	George Wilson literally blends in with his surroundings. He lacks the immediacy of the physical charisma that Tom has. George is weak, ghost-like, impotent.
Myrtle	"the thickish figure of a woman blocked out the light from the office door. She was in the middle thirties, and faintly stout, but she carried her surplus flesh sensuously as some women can"	"Her face, above a spotted dress of dark blue crepe-de-chine, contained no facet or gleam of beauty, but there was an immediately perceptible vitality about her as if the nerves of her body were continually smouldering"	"Mrs. Wilson had changed her costume some time before, and was now attired in an elaborate afternoon dress of cream-colored chiffon, which gave out a continual rustle as she swept about the room. With the influence of the dress her personality had also undergone a change. The intense vitality that had been so remarkable in the garage was converted into impressive hauteur"	

The Great Gatsby Chapters 1-2

Reading Activity 4: Action, Character, Decision

Anchor Standard	**11th-12th Grade**
CCRA.R.1	RL.11-12.1
CCRA.SL.1	SL.11-12.1

Objective

Students will identify particular lines of dialogue or incidents in the story that propel the action, reveal aspects of character, or provoke a decision.

Directions

The following page contains passages from the chapters 1-2 of *The Great Gatsby*. Students should determine whether the passages advance the action, reveal aspects of a character, or provoke a decision.

This can be done as a whole-class activity, individually, or in small groups.

Follow-Up/Assessment/Extension

Have students skim chapters 1-2 in the text to find one example of a passage that propels the action, one that reveals aspects of a character, and one that provokes a decision. Again, this could be done individually or as a group. This activity can be a quick prompt for starting class discussion of a reading assignment.

The Great Gatsby Chapters 1-2: Action, Character, Decision

Write **A** (for Action) **C** (for Character) or **D** (for Decision) in the blank next to each to identify whether the passage/statement advances the action, tells us more about a character, or provokes a decision. On the lines under each question, provide a short explanation of your choice.

___ 1. Reserving judgments is a matter of infinite hope. I am still a little afraid of missing something if I forget that, as my father snobbishly suggested, and I snobbishly repeat, a sense of the fundamental decencies is parceled out unequally at birth.

___ 2. "Gatsby?" demanded Daisy. "What Gatsby?"

___ 3. "Civilization's going to pieces," broke out Tom violently. "I've gotten to be a terrible pessimist about things. Have you read 'The Rise of the Colored Empires' by this man Goddard?".

___ 4. The bottle of whiskey — a second one — was now in constant demand by all present, excepting Catherine, who "felt just as good on nothing at all."

___ 5. Daisy! Daisy! Daisy!" shouted Mrs. Wilson. "I'll say it whenever I want to! Daisy! Dai —"

The Great Gatsby Chapters 1-2:
Action, Character, Decision Suggested Answers

Write **A** (for Action) **C** (for Character) or **D** (for Decision) in the blank next to each to identify whether the passage/statement advances the action, tells us more about a character, or provokes a decision. On the lines under each question, provide a short explanation of your choice.

C 1. Reserving judgments is a matter of infinite hope. I am still a little afraid of missing something if I forget that, as my father snobbishly suggested, and I snobbishly repeat, a sense of the fundamental decencies is parceled out unequally at birth.

This passage explains Nick's worldview and how he sets out to avoid judging people. However, the passage shows that Nick is aware of his own irony—that the thought itself is "snobbish."

A 2. "Gatsby?" demanded Daisy. "What Gatsby?"

Daisy's recognition of Gatsby's name—and her immediate desperate interest ("demanded") sets the reader up for the primary plot development of the novel, Daisy's reunion with Gatsby.

C 3. "Civilization's going to pieces," broke out Tom violently. "I've gotten to be a terrible pessimist about things. Have you read 'The Rise of the Colored Empires' by this man Goddard?"

This passage suggests that Tom is hotly opinionated ("violently"), and is racist as well as classist.

A 4. The bottle of whiskey — a second one — was now in constant demand by all present, excepting Catherine, who "felt just as good on nothing at all."

Alcohol—and what happens when one does or does not drink it to excess—is a recurrent motif in the novel. Alcohol advances the action taken at this party, including Tom's violence toward Myrtle. Nick notes that this was only the second time he had been drunk in his life.

D 5. Daisy! Daisy! Daisy!" shouted Mrs. Wilson. "I'll say it whenever I want to! Daisy! Dai —"

Upon hearing Myrtle disobediently saying Daisy's name to deliberately challenge and provoke Tom, he immediately makes a decision to strike Myrtle.

The Great Gatsby Chapters 1-2

Reading Activity 5: Figurative Language

Anchor Standard	11th-12th Grade
CCRA.R.4	RL.11-12.4
CCRA.SL.1	SL.11-12.1

Objectives

- Students will determine the meaning of words and phrases as they are used in the text, including figurative and connotative meanings.
- Students will determine whether passages from the text that include botanical imagery, a major motif in the novel, are being used literally or figuratively.

Directions

The following page has passages from the text that include botanical imagery and references which are used literally or figuratively. This worksheet can be done individually, as a whole-class activity, or in small groups. Discuss the answers as a whole class. Collect the worksheets and record the grades if you choose to do so.

Follow-Up/Assessment/Extension

Ask students to begin tracking instances of botanical allusions. As students observe these occurrences, ask them to think about which characters are most associated with these allusions. Discuss what these associations reveal about the characters.

The Great Gatsby Chapters 1-2: Figurative Language

On the short line provided, write **F** for figurative or **L** for literal. On the lines under each question, explain how the botanical reference or imagery helps create meaning.

___ 1. And so with the sunshine and the great bursts of leaves growing on the trees, just as things grow in fast movies, I had that familiar conviction that life was beginning over again with the summer.

___ 2. The lawn started at the beach and ran toward the front door for a quarter of a mile, jumping over sun-dials and brick walks and burning gardens — finally when it reached the house drifting up the side in bright vines as though from the momentum of its run.

___ 3. Turning me around by one arm, he moved a broad flat hand along the front vista, including in its sweep a sunken Italian garden, a half-acre of deep, pungent roses, and a snub-nosed motor-boat that bumped the tide offshore.

___ 4. We walked through a high hallway into a bright rosy-colored space, fragilely bound into the house by French windows at either end.

___ 5. The whole town is desolate. All the cars have the left rear wheel painted black as a mourning wreath, and there's a persistent wail all night along the north shore."

___ 6. Inside, the crimson room bloomed with light.

___ 7. But we heard it," insisted Daisy, surprising me by opening up again in a flower-like way. "We heard it from three people, so it must be true."

____ 8. "I love to see you at my table, Nick. You remind me of a — of a rose, an absolute rose. Doesn't he?" She turned to Miss Baker for confirmation: "An absolute rose?"
This was untrue. I am not even faintly like a rose. She was only extemporizing, but a stirring warmth flowed from her, as if her heart was trying to come out to you concealed in one of those breathless, thrilling words.

____ 9. The lamp-light, bright on his boots and dull on the autumn-leaf yellow of her hair, glinted along the paper as she turned a page with a flutter of slender muscles in her arms.

____ 10. The late afternoon sky bloomed in the window for a moment like the blue honey of the Mediterranean — then the shrill voice of Mrs. McKee called me back into the room.

The Great Gatsby Chapters 1-2: Figurative Language Suggested Answers

On the short line provided, write **F** for figurative or **L** for literal. On the lines under each question, explain how the botanical reference or imagery helps create meaning.

F 1. And so with the sunshine and the great bursts of leaves growing on the trees, just as things grow in fast movies, I had that familiar conviction that life was beginning over again with the summer.
The reference to "leaves" is an unnatural one, they "burst." The speaker also explains how the leaves he refers to are cinematic—they are more artificial than they are real.

F 2. The lawn started at the beach and ran toward the front door for a quarter of a mile, jumping over sun-dials and brick walks and burning gardens — finally when it reached the house drifting up the side in bright vines as though from the momentum of its run.
The lawn is given anthropomorphized qualities ("ran," "jump") and the description of it conveys how huge it is, connoting the vast wealth that the Buchanans have.

L 3. Turning me around by one arm, he moved a broad flat hand along the front vista, including in its sweep a sunken Italian garden, a half-acre of deep, pungent roses, and a snub-nosed motor-boat that bumped the tide offshore.
The use is literal, and interestingly uses roses and a boat as status symbols of wealth.

L 4. We walked through a high hallway into a bright rosy-colored space, fragilely bound into the house by French windows at either end.
Though a descriptor, it is presumably literal, and still has connotations of being positive (i.e. "rose colored").

F 5. The whole town is desolate. All the cars have the left rear wheel painted black as a mourning wreath, and there's a persistent wail all night along the north shore."
Here the reference to "a mourning wreath" is a simile. The reference is an exaggeration to convey how much Daisy is missed in the Midwest. The allusion to a funeral is ominous.

F 6. Inside, the crimson room bloomed with light.
The botanical reference is a metaphor. A room or light do not generally "bloom," but here it connotes a beginning, like the bloom of a flower.

F 7. But we heard it," insisted Daisy, surprising me by opening up again in a flower-like way. "We heard it from three people, so it must be true."
The comparison of how Daisy relates to others as a flower opening suggests that she is similar to a flower: beautiful, fragile, temporary, and an object to be looked at and admired.

F 8. "I love to see you at my table, Nick. You remind me of a — of a rose, an absolute rose. Doesn't he?" She turned to Miss Baker for confirmation: "An absolute rose?"
This was untrue. I am not even faintly like a rose. She was only extemporizing, but a stirring warmth flowed from her, as if her heart was trying to come out to you concealed in one of those breathless, thrilling words.
Daisy makes an attempt to be metaphorical, but Nick (as narrator) rejects Daisy's estimation of him. A rose is beautiful and delicate, yet has thorns—this does not seem to suit Nick.

L 9. The lamp-light, bright on his boots and dull on the autumn-leaf yellow of her hair, glinted along the paper as she turned a page with a flutter of slender muscles in her arms.
Though a descriptor, it is presumably literal, connects Jordan to a different season than the one the story is currently set in (spring), associating her with fall instead.

F 10. The late afternoon sky bloomed in the window for a moment like the blue honey of the Mediterranean — then the shrill voice of Mrs. McKee called me back into the room.
The sky is described using a botanical term. The description is attributed to the narrator, who explains that that is what he notices until he is brought back into the present moment by the interruption caused by Mrs. McKee. The comparison suggests that Nick (who claims to reserve judging people) does not like her.

The Great Gatsby Chapters 1-2

Reading Activity 6: Elements of Fiction & Literary Devices

Anchor Standard	11th-12th Grade
CCRA.R.1	RL.11-12.1
	RL.11-12.2
	RL.11-12.4
	RL.11-12.5
CCRA.SL.1	SL.11-12.1

Objective

Students will study and discuss passages from the text to examine how setting and its significance creates meaning in the text.

Directions

Use the following passages and discussion questions as a guide to discussing how setting is significant in creating meaning in the novel. You can give students the questions ahead of time and have them formulate answers prior to the class discussion or you can jump right in with a whole class discussion without student preparation if your students will handle that well.

As you hold the class discussion, be sure to include conversations defining setting as a function of both time and place, and how these work together to advance meaning in the text.

Follow-Up/Assessment/Extension

After your discussion, ask students to look for recurrences East vs. West Egg in future chapters, and consider how this tension defines and divides characters in the novel.

The Great Gatsby Chapters 1-2: Elements of Fiction & Literary Devices

1. "When I came back from the East last autumn I felt that I wanted the world to be in uniform and at a sort of moral attention forever; I wanted no more riotous excursions with privileged glimpses into the human heart."

   What is "the East" associated with here?

2. "My family have been prominent, well-to-do people in this Middle Western city for three generations. The Carraways are something of a clan, and we have a tradition that we're descended from the Dukes of Buccleuch, but the actual founder of my line was my grandfather's brother, who came here in fifty-one, sent a substitute to the Civil War, and started the wholesale hardware business that my father carries on to-day."

   What qualities do the Carraways of the "Middle West" have?

3. "It was lonely for a day or so until one morning some man, more recently arrived than I, stopped me on the road.
'How do you get to West Egg village?' he asked helplessly.
I told him. And as I walked on I was lonely no longer. I was a guide, a pathfinder, an original settler. He had casually conferred on me the freedom of the neighborhood."

How does Nick's relationship to setting change? Why is that significant?

4. Instead of being the warm center of the world, the Middle West now seemed like the ragged edge of the universe — so I decided to go East and learn the bond business. Everybody I knew was in the bond business, so I supposed it could support one more single man. All my aunts and uncles talked it over as if they were choosing a prep school for me, and finally said, "Why — ye — es," with very grave, hesitant faces. Father agreed to finance me for a year, and after various delays I came East, permanently, I thought, in the spring of twenty-two."

What associations does Nick have with "the East"?

5. "It was a matter of chance that I should have rented a house in one of the strangest communities in North America. It was on that slender riotous island which extends itself due east of New York — and where there are, among other natural curiosities, two unusual formations of land. Twenty miles from the city a pair of enormous eggs, identical in contour and separated only by a courtesy bay, jut out into the most domesticated body of salt water in the Western hemisphere, the great wet barnyard of Long Island Sound. They are not perfect ovals — like the egg in the Columbus story, they are both crushed flat at the contact end — but their physical resemblance must be a source of perpetual confusion to the gulls that fly overhead. To the wingless a more arresting phenomenon is their dissimilarity in every particular except shape and size."

   What are the physical qualities of the land—what contradiction does Nick point out?

6. "I lived at West Egg, the – well, the least fashionable of the two, though this is a most superficial tag to express the bizarre and not a little sinister contrast between them. My house was at the very tip of the egg, only fifty yards from the Sound, and squeezed between two huge places that rented for twelve or fifteen thousand a season. The one on my right was a colossal affair by any standard ... My own house was an eyesore, but it was a small eyesore, and it had been overlooked, so I had a view of the water, a partial view of my neighbor's lawn, and the consoling proximity of millionaires—all for eighty dollars a month."

   What is the difference between the two "Eggs," according to Nick?

7. "When they do get married," continued Catherine, "they're going West to live for a while until it blows over."

What is associated with the "West" in the passage?

The Great Gatsby Chapters 1-2:
Elements of Fiction & Literary Devices Suggested Answers

1. "When I came back from the East last autumn I felt that I wanted the world to be in uniform and at a sort of moral attention forever; I wanted no more riotous excursions with privileged glimpses into the human heart."

   What is "the East" associated with here?
   "The East" is the opposite of what Nick seeks ("the world to be in uniform and at a sort of moral attention"), it is "riotous" and associated with his tumultuous and emotional experiences connected with his association to Gatsby.

2. "My family have been prominent, well-to-do people in this Middle Western city for three generations. The Carraways are something of a clan, and we have a tradition that we're descended from the Dukes of Buccleuch, but the actual founder of my line was my grandfather's brother, who came here in fifty-one, sent a substitute to the Civil War, and started the wholesale hardware business that my father carries on to-day."

   What qualities do the Carraways of the "Middle West" have?
   First, they are settlers, not original inhabitants, but established over generations. The family perpetuates a mythology of their connection to place, but the truth of their residency is not royal ("Dukes"), but very pedestrian ("wholesale hardware business").

3. "It was lonely for a day or so until one morning some man, more recently arrived than I, stopped me on the road.

   'How do you get to West Egg village?' he asked helplessly.

   I told him. And as I walked on I was lonely no longer. I was a guide, a pathfinder, an original settler. He had casually conferred on me the freedom of the neighborhood."

   How does Nick's relationship to setting change? Why is that significant?
   Nick's view of himself as an inhabitant changes—he is no longer an outsider, but a member. Of course he is not "an original settler," so he adopts a romantic mythology (similar to how Gatsby does).

4. "Instead of being the warm center of the world, the Middle West now seemed like the ragged edge of the universe — so I decided to go East and learn the bond business. Everybody I knew was in the bond business, so I supposed it could support one more single man. All my aunts and uncles talked it over as if they were choosing a prep school for me, and finally said, "Why — ye — es," with very grave, hesitant faces. Father agreed to finance me for a year, and after various delays I came East, permanently, I thought, in the spring of twenty-two."

What associations does Nick have with "the East"?
Nick no longer associated his home ("the Middle West") positively—rather it is "ragged," perhaps parochial after his experiences abroad as a soldier. Going "East"—to a major metropolis—represents possibility. Nick adds that his beliefs were not realized.

5. "It was a matter of chance that I should have rented a house in one of the strangest communities in North America. It was on that slender riotous island which extends itself due east of New York — and where there are, among other natural curiosities, two unusual formations of land. Twenty miles from the city a pair of enormous eggs, identical in contour and separated only by a courtesy bay, jut out into the most domesticated body of salt water in the Western hemisphere, the great wet barnyard of Long Island Sound. They are not perfect ovals — like the egg in the Columbus story, they are both crushed flat at the contact end — but their physical resemblance must be a source of perpetual confusion to the gulls that fly overhead. To the wingless a more arresting phenomenon is their dissimilarity in every particular except shape and size."

   What are the physical qualities of the land—what contradiction does Nick point out?
   It has a "pair of enormous eggs." They are "unusual," and "identical" *but only to gulls.* They share the same shape and size, but, from the perspective of those on land, they are very different in most ways. Symbolically, we're being told that the eggs represent the people who live in East Egg and West Egg. When the gulls fly over and see the people in both locations, they see them as essentially the same—they're people. However when the people ("wingless") view each other, they appear to be quite different to each other based on wealth and social status.

6. "I lived at West Egg, the – well, the least fashionable of the two, though this is a most superficial tag to express the bizarre and not a little sinister contrast between them. My house was at the very tip of the egg, only fifty yards from the Sound, and squeezed between two huge places that rented for twelve or fifteen thousand a season. The one on my right was a colossal affair by any standard … My own house was an eyesore, but it was a small eyesore, and it had been overlooked, so I had a view of the water, a partial view of my neighbor's lawn, and the consoling proximity of millionaires—all for eighty dollars a month."

   What is the difference between the two "Eggs," according to Nick?
   The West Egg is "the least fashionable," but the "contrast" is "bizarre" and "not a little sinister," which suggests that there is animosity between the two areas.

7. "When they do get married," continued Catherine, "they're going West to live for a while until it blows over."

   What is associated with the "West" in the passage?
   The "West" is associated with new beginnings and anonymity, as well as the freedom from social scrutiny so one can do whatever one pleases, even if it is against social graces (i.e. divorce and marrying one's mistress).

The Great Gatsby Chapters 1-2

Reading Activity 7: Meaning and Inferences

Anchor Standard	11th-12th Grade
CCRA.R.1	RL.11-12.1
CCRA.SL.1	SL.11-12.1

Objective

Students will answer questions about selected passages from the text which require them to extract meaning or inferences from the text.

Directions

The following pages contain passages from chapters 1-2 of *The Great Gatsby* and questions related to the passages that require close reading to answer. Students should answer the questions related to the passages.

This can be done as a whole-class activity, individually, or in small groups. If it is done individually or in small groups, come together as a class to discuss the answers to the questions.

Follow-Up/Assessment/Extension

Collect the worksheets for review and/or grading. Ask students to keep these as possible raw material for writing essays in the future.

The Great Gatsby Chapters 1-2: Meaning & Inferences 1

Read the passages and answer the related questions.

1. *No — Gatsby turned out all right at the end; it is what preyed on Gatsby, what foul dust floated in the wake of his dreams that temporarily closed out my interest in the abortive sorrows and short-winded elations of men.*

According to Nick, what caused him to become introverted?

2. *Her husband, among various physical accomplishments, had been one of the most powerful ends that ever played football at New Haven — a national figure in a way, one of those men who reach such an acute limited excellence at twenty-one that everything afterward savors of anti-climax. His family were enormously wealthy — even in college his freedom with money was a matter for reproach — but now he'd left Chicago and come East in a fashion that rather took your breath away: for instance, he'd brought down a string of polo ponies from Lake Forest. It was hard to realize that a man in my own generation was wealthy enough to do that.*

What is Nick's impression of Tom?

3. *For a moment the last sunshine fell with romantic affection upon her glowing face; her voice compelled me forward breathlessly as I listened — then the glow faded, each light deserting her with lingering regret, like children leaving a pleasant street at dusk.*

What does this description suggest about Daisy's state?

4. *So Tom Buchanan and his girl and I went up together to New York — or not quite together, for Mrs. Wilson sat discreetly in another car. Tom deferred that much to the sensibilities of those East Eggers who might be on the train.*

What does this suggest about Tom?

5. *We went on, cutting back again over the Park toward the West Hundreds. At 158th Street the cab stopped at one slice in a long white cake of apartment-houses. Throwing a regal homecoming glance around the neighborhood, Mrs. Wilson gathered up her dog and her other purchases, and went haughtily in.*

What does this passage reveal about Myrtle?

The Great Gatsby Chapters 1-2: Meaning & Inferences 1 Suggested Answers

Read the passages and answer the related questions.

1. *No — Gatsby turned out all right at the end; it is what preyed on Gatsby, what foul dust floated in the wake of his dreams that temporarily closed out my interest in the abortive sorrows and short-winded elations of men.*

According to Nick, what caused him to become introverted?

What Nick observed after the incident involving Gatsby is what caused him to withdraw from other people, specifically the way people "preyed" on Gatsby.

2. *Her husband, among various physical accomplishments, had been one of the most powerful ends that ever played football at New Haven — a national figure in a way, one of those men who reach such an acute limited excellence at twenty-one that everything afterward savors of anti-climax. His family were enormously wealthy — even in college his freedom with money was a matter for reproach — but now he'd left Chicago and come East in a fashion that rather took your breath away: for instance, he'd brought down a string of polo ponies from Lake Forest. It was hard to realize that a man in my own generation was wealthy enough to do that.*

What is Nick's impression of Tom?

Ultimately Nick is impressed by Tom's wealth and power ("took your breath away"). There is a connection, from Nick's perspective, between Tom's wealth and his impressiveness. Nick seems simultaneously repulsed and fascinated by it.

3. *For a moment the last sunshine fell with romantic affection upon her glowing face; her voice compelled me forward breathlessly as I listened — then the glow faded, each light deserting her with lingering regret, like children leaving a pleasant street at dusk.*

What does this description suggest about Daisy's state?

It suggests that Daisy's happiness is at best temporary, but likely feigned. She is capable of being charming and beguiling, but it is not a permanent state, because she is actually quite sad and disappointed (like children who must go in at dark).

4. *So Tom Buchanan and his girl and I went up together to New York — or not quite together, for Mrs. Wilson sat discreetly in another car. Tom deferred that much to the sensibilities of those East Eggers who might be on the train.*

What does this suggest about Tom?

Tom, despite his wealth and power, must adhere to social conventions and graces by hiding his infidelities.

5. *We went on, cutting back again over the Park toward the West Hundreds. At 158th Street the cab stopped at one slice in a long white cake of apartment-houses. Throwing a regal homecoming glance around the neighborhood, Mrs. Wilson gathered up her dog and her other purchases, and went haughtily in.*

What does this passage reveal about Myrtle?

The passage shows how Myrtle is materialistic. She is the wife of a largely unsuccessful gas-station owner, a life she feels is not genuine or appropriate for her. Her real "home" is this apartment ("homecoming glance") and it, along with objects she bought, give her a secured sense of class ("haughty").

The Great Gatsby Chapters 1-2: Meaning & Inferences 2

Read the passage and answer the related questions.

About half way between West Egg and New York the motor road hastily joins the railroad and runs beside it for a quarter of a mile, so as to shrink away from a certain desolate area of land. This is a valley of ashes — a fantastic farm where ashes grow like wheat into ridges and hills and grotesque gardens; where ashes take the forms of houses and chimneys and rising smoke and, finally, with a transcendent effort, of men who move dimly and already crumbling through the powdery air. Occasionally a line of gray cars crawls along an invisible track, gives out a ghastly creak, and comes to rest, and immediately the ash-gray men swarm up with leaden spades and stir up an impenetrable cloud, which screens their obscure operations from your sight. But above the gray land and the spasms of bleak dust which drift endlessly over it, you perceive, after a moment, the eyes of Doctor T. J. Eckleburg. The eyes of Doctor T. J. Eckleburg are blue and gigantic — their irises are one yard high. They look out of no face, but, instead, from a pair of enormous yellow spectacles which pass over a nonexistent nose. Evidently some wild wag of an oculist set them there to fatten his practice in the borough of Queens, and then sank down himself into eternal blindness, or forgot them and moved away. But his eyes, dimmed a little by many paintless days, under sun and rain, brood on over the solemn dumping ground.

1. What is the significance of the use of the word "farm?" Why is it ironic?

2. What color are the men? Why is this significant?

3. Who is T.J. Eckleburg? What, according to the narrator, was the purpose of the billboard? Why is that significant, given its location?

4. Why is the position of the billboard's "eyes" significant?

5. What does the valley of ashes look like? What does it represent?

The Great Gatsby Chapters 1-2: Meaning & Inferences 2 Suggested Answers

Read the passage and answer the related questions.

About half way between West Egg and New York the motor road hastily joins the railroad and runs beside it for a quarter of a mile, so as to shrink away from a certain desolate area of land. This is a valley of ashes — a fantastic farm where ashes grow like wheat into ridges and hills and grotesque gardens; where ashes take the forms of houses and chimneys and rising smoke and, finally, with a transcendent effort, of men who move dimly and already crumbling through the powdery air. Occasionally a line of gray cars crawls along an invisible track, gives out a ghastly creak, and comes to rest, and immediately the ash-gray men swarm up with leaden spades and stir up an impenetrable cloud, which screens their obscure operations from your sight. But above the gray land and the spasms of bleak dust which drift endlessly over it, you perceive, after a moment, the eyes of Doctor T. J. Eckleburg. The eyes of Doctor T. J. Eckleburg are blue and gigantic — their irises are one yard high. They look out of no face, but, instead, from a pair of enormous yellow spectacles which pass over a nonexistent nose. Evidently some wild wag of an oculist set them there to fatten his practice in the borough of Queens, and then sank down himself into eternal blindness, or forgot them and moved away. But his eyes, dimmed a little by many paintless days, under sun and rain, brood on over the solemn dumping ground.

1. What is the significance of the use of the word "farm?" Why is it ironic?
A farm is a place where growth and production are deliberate because the end products have use. The ashes are the consequence of industrial production, a negative side effect. No one would grow ashes deliberately.

2. What color are the men? Why is this significant?
The workers are "ash-gray," which shows that they are so affected by the environment that they eventually blend into it. Individual identity is lost because they are poor workers, not elites. George Wilson is also described as gray.

3. Who is T.J. Eckleburg? What, according to the narrator, was the purpose of the billboard? Why is that significant, given its location?
T.J. Eckleburg is an optometrist. According to the narrator, the billboard's creation and placement was motivated by economic gain, "to fatten up his practice." The practice is in the city, yet the billboard is in the "valley of ashes," forgotten and dilapidated—a place where finding fat wallets to fatten a practice is unlikely. In a way, it is a statement about socioeconomic difference.

4. Why is the position of the billboard's "eyes" significant?
The eyes "brood [over]" the area, with a perspective that is omniscient. T,J. Eckleburg sees everything that happens in the valley of ashes. The elite—represented by the eye doctor—look down on the ash-gray workers.

5. What does the valley of ashes look like? What does it represent?
The area is gray, lifeless and ghostly, existing only as a dumping ground for ashes from the city. It is a contrast to the opulence of the city, literally a place for its refuse. It is a place where the wealthy and privileged would not live, but where the poor have to.

The Great Gatsby Chapters 1-2

Writing Activity 1: How Do Men Relate to One Another?

Anchor Standard	11th-12th Grade
CCRA.SL.1	SL.11-12.1, 1a-1d
CCRA.SL.3	SL. 11-12.4
CCRA.W.1	W. 11-12.2
CCRA.W.2	W. 11-12.4
CCRA.W.4	W. 11-12.5
CCRA.W.5	W. 11-12.7
	W. 11-12.9, 9b

Objectives

- Students will evaluate and analyze textual evidence to determine how men relate to one another through words and behaviors.
- Students will evaluate passages about male characters to observe how patterns of interaction may be related to deeper meanings and themes in the novel.
- Students will compare and contrast Tom and Nick, and their words and behaviors towards other men.
- Students will write a composition in which they consider their analysis of these interactions to answer the question, "How do men relate to one another?"

Directions

The following series of worksheets and information organizers can be used by students individually, in small groups, or done partly as a whole-class activity. They are intended to guide students through the process of reading and thinking critically about information by ultimately answering the single question, "How do men relate to one another?

Preview the following pages. Determine the best way to have your particular class handle this assignment (individually, pairs, groups, whole-class, or some combination). A combination of group work (to do the analyzing of the text on the chart page) followed by individual work (to do the second and third pages of the assignment) would most likely be best to fulfill the standards listed for this assignment.

Follow-Up/Assessment/Extension

- The written assignment will be a good basis for assessment of the students' success with this assignment. Create a rubric explaining the criteria on which their written assignments will be evaluated.
- Tell students to continue observing ways that masculinity is expressed in interactions between men only and between men and women.
- Have some students read/present their writing assignments to the class to practice more speaking/listening skills and to expose all students to each other's' ideas.
- Use this assignment to introduce these themes: power, class, and masculinity.

The Great Gatsby Chapters 1-2: How Do Men Relate to One Another?

In chapters 1-2, masculinity as a concept is explored primarily through Tom, and to a lesser extent Nick, as well as some minor characters.

The ways in which characters interact fuel a narrative by advancing conflict and therefore plot. *The Great Gatsby* is very much a novel about masculine identity and its prerogatives. This is apparent in how men interact with one another.

Using textual evidence from chapters 1-2, look for patterns to begin formulating an answer to the question "How do men relate to one another?". As you develop an answer, consider why it is significant. What do these relationship dynamics reveal about the characters? How do they create meaning in the novel?

To determine an idea about how men relate to one another:

1. Identify passages and quotes where Nick and Tom interact with other male characters.

2. Examine the context of your quotes.

3. Consider the connotation and denotation of key phrases in your quotes.

    a. What is the tone—friendly, adversarial, angry, competitive?
    b. Is there a conflict?
    c. What attitudes are the characters revealing or concealing in their language?

4. Look for patterns in your evidence. Is a word or idea repeated? Use these patterns to shape an answer to the question.

The Great Gatsby Chapters 1-2: How Do Men Relate to One Another?

Complete the chart to analyze information to develop ideas to write your essay.

Character	Quote/passage interacting with Nick	Quote/passage interacting with Tom	Observations
Tom		N/A	
Nick	N/A		
Wilson			
Dog Seller			
McKee			

The Great Gatsby Chapters 1-2
Suggested Writing Assignments

Anchor Standard	11th-12th Grade
CCRA.W.1	W.11-12.1, 1a-1e
CCRA W.2	W.11-12.2, 2a-2f
CCRA.W.3	W.11-12.3, 3a-3e
CCRA.W.4	W.11-12.4
CCRA.W.5	W. 11-12.5

Objective
Students will be assigned or will choose one of a selection of writing assignments pertaining to chapters 1-2 of *The Great Gatsby* to fulfill one or more of the standards listed above.

Directions
To provide you with maximum flexibility for differentiated instruction, the following page has a list of suggested writing assignments, all related to Chapters 1-2 of *The Great Gatsby*. Either assign individual students particular assignments to do or allow students to choose their own assignments.

A second page of "Quick Write" topics is also included.

Follow-Up/Assessment/Extension
- Have dramatic readings of students' narratives or poems.
- Create a "reading room" space in your classroom where students can donate their writing assignments for others in the class to read.
- Allow students to do more than one assignment if they want to.
- Use the "left-over" assignments (not chosen for this activity) as topics for journal entries.

The Great Gatsby Chapters 1-2: Creative Analytical Writing Assignments

1. Write a business plan by George Wilson for improving his gas station business, including how he would like to sell used cars and cater to more upscale clientele.

2. Write a flashback to when Daisy and Jordan first met and became friends.

3. Write a letter from Nick to his father, sent while Nick was a soldier in World War I.

4. Write a "solemn and obvious" editorial by Nick for the *Yale News*.

5. Choose a section of text from the dinner party scene in chapter 1 and write a meta-narrative of what a character is really thinking.

6. Write a love letter from Myrtle to Tom.

7. Write a paragraph describing what T.J. Eckleburg "sees."

8. Imagine that Jordan Baker keeps a diary. Write an entry that describes her first encounter with Nick.

9. Write scene with dialogue where Tom apologizes to Myrtle for striking her.

10. An ellipsis is a form of punctuation that signifies omission. At the end of chapter 2, locate the sentence: "...I was standing beside his bed and he was sitting up..." Write a paragraph describing what you imagine occurred (and Fitzgerald omitted) just before that sentence begins.

The Great Gatsby Chapters 1-2: Quick-Write Writing Assignments

1. Does Nick find Jordan attractive? What about her interests him?
2. How has being a soldier in World War I affected Nick?
3. Does Daisy overreact to receiving phone calls from Tom's "woman in New York"?
4. Does Gatsby have a mystical or magical quality to him? Describe it.
5. Is Nick a trustworthy narrator?
6. Nick claims that he reserves judgment of other people. Whether he does or not, in what ways could the characters be judged?
7. Why the emphasis on sports (football, polo) around Tom? What does this reveal about his character?
8. Is the gathering at Tom and Myrtle's apartment fun at all? If so, how? If not, why not?
9. Most of the characters in the novel are materialistic and obsessed with stuff. Which character seems most obsessed with things?
10. What is the novel suggesting so far about marriage? Is it a sacred bond?

MATERIALS: CHAPTER 3
THE GREAT GATSBY

Reading Activity 1: True or False

Reading Activity 2: Analyzing Passages

Reading Activity 3: Minor Characters

Reading Activity 4: Action, Character, Decision

Reading Activity 5: Figurative Language

Reading Activity 6: Elements of Fiction & Literary Devices

Reading Activity 7: Meaning and Inferences

Writing Activity 1: Who Is Gatsby?

Suggested Writing Assignments

Quick-Write Assignments

NOTES
THE GREAT GATSBY

The Great Gatsby Chapter 3

Reading Activity 1: True or False?

Anchor Standard	11th-12th Grade
CCRA.R.1	RL.11-12.1
CCRA.SL1	SL.11-12.1
CCRA SL.4	SL.11-12.4

Objectives

- Students will be able to cite the parts of the text that support their analysis of what the text says or infers
- Students will consider statements about the text, determine whether those statements are true or false, and will give textual evidence supporting their choices
- Students will work together in small groups to discuss, analyze, and evaluate the statements made
- Students will evaluate the analytical work of their peers

Directions

Prior to reading Chapter 3: Give students (or post) the following list of statements about the chapters, and explain to students that they should read Chapter 3 to find out if these statements are true or false:

Gatsby is famous in New York because of the lavish parties he throws each weekend.
Gatsby and Nick are both veterans of World War II.
Nick claims that he is a dishonest person.
Nick drinks a lot at Gatsby's party.
Nick is in love with Jordan Baker.
Jordan prefers simpler, unobservant men as sutors.

After reading Chapter 3: The worksheets on the following pages can be done by students individually, in small groups, or as a whole class. Below are directions to use the questions as a group activity to fulfill more state standards:

- Cut the worksheet apart, making each question and answer box a slip.
- Divide your class into six groups and give one question and a True/False evaluation form to each group. Tell students they are to discuss the statement and determine if the statement is true or false, supporting their decision with evidence from the text. Tell them their answers will be evaluated on the criteria given on the evaluation form.
- Give students ample time to discuss the statements and record their answers.
- Have the groups swap True or False question slips so that each group can evaluate another group's answer. The group should fill in the number of the question they are evaluating, decide how well the answer fulfills the criteria listed, and fill out the form accordingly.
- Repeat the previous step until all the groups have evaluated each others' answers.
- Collect the evaluations and answer slips.

The Great Gatsby Chapter 3: True or False?

Write *True* or *False* in the blank next to each statement. Below the statement, explain why you chose true or false, referencing the text to support your choices.

_________ 1. Gatsby is famous in New York because of the lavish parties he throws each weekend.

_________ 2. Gatsby and Nick are both veterans of World War II.

_________ 3. Nick claims that he is a dishonest person.

_________ 4. Nick drinks a lot at Gatsby's party.

__________ 5. Nick is in love with Jordan Baker.

__________ 6. Jordan prefers simpler, unobservant men as suitors.

The Great Gatsby Chapter 3 True or False? Evaluation

List Your Group's Members: Your Group's Question # _______

__________________ __________________ __________________

__________________ __________________ __________________

1 = No, Not At All **2** = A Little **3** = Some **4** = Yes **5** = Yes, Very Well

Evaluation of Question # ___
Does the explanation support the answer of true or false? 1 2 3 4 5
Is there good textual evidence to support the answer? 1 2 3 4 5
Is the answer clearly stated? 1 2 3 4 5
Total Score ________ of a possible 15 points

Evaluation of Question # ___
Does the explanation support the answer of true or false? 1 2 3 4 5
Is there good textual evidence to support the answer? 1 2 3 4 5
Is the answer clearly stated? 1 2 3 4 5
Total Score ________ of a possible 15 points

Evaluation of Question # ___
Does the explanation support the answer of true or false? 1 2 3 4 5
Is there good textual evidence to support the answer? 1 2 3 4 5
Is the answer clearly stated? 1 2 3 4 5
Total Score ________ of a possible 15 points

Evaluation of Question # ___
Does the explanation support the answer of true or false? 1 2 3 4 5
Is there good textual evidence to support the answer? 1 2 3 4 5
Is the answer clearly stated? 1 2 3 4 5
Total Score ________ of a possible 15 points

Evaluation of Question # ___
Does the explanation support the answer of true or false? 1 2 3 4 5
Is there good textual evidence to support the answer? 1 2 3 4 5
Is the answer clearly stated? 1 2 3 4 5
Total Score ________ of a possible 15 points

The Great Gatsby Chapter 3: True or False? Suggested Answers

Write *True* or *False* in the blank next to each statement. Below the statement, explain why you chose true or false, referencing the text to support your choices.

TRUE 1. Gatsby is famous in New York because of the lavish parties he throws each weekend.

Nick is personally invited, yet he does not know Gatsby. Gatsby's parties are infamous, but they are not social gatherings in the sense that Gatsby wants to socialize with his friends. Rather, Nick remarks, "I believe that on the first night I went to Gatsby's house I was one of the few guests who had actually been invited. People were not invited — they went there." Gatsby is famous for throwing parties but, ironically, is a personally unknown figure to most of his guests—and is frequently the subject of their gossip.

TRUE 2. Gatsby and Nick are both veterans of World War II.

Gatsby recognizes Nick first: "Your face is familiar," he said, politely. "Weren't you in the Third Division during the war?" Nick confirms that he was also in France during the war.

FALSE 3. Nick claims that he is a dishonest person.

Nick believes that Jordan is dishonest, but he is the opposite: "Every one suspects himself of at least one of the cardinal virtues, and this is mine: I am one of the few honest people that I have ever known."

TRUE 4. Nick drinks a lot at Gatsby's party.

Overcoming his anxiety about not knowing his host, Nick decides to relax his inhibitions and begins drinking: I was enjoying myself now. I had taken two finger-bowls of champagne, and the scene had changed before my eyes into something significant, elemental, and profound.

FALSE 5. Nick is in love with Jordan Baker.

Though Nick considers for a moment that he might be in love with her, he is not: "I wasn't actually in love, but I felt a sort of tender curiosity."

TRUE 6. Jordan prefers simpler, unobservant men as suitors.

Because of her propensity for dishonesty, according to the narrator: "Jordan Baker instinctively avoided clever, shrewd men, and now I saw that this was because she felt safer on a plane where any divergence from a code would be thought impossible."

The Great Gatsby Chapter 3

Reading Activity 2: Analyzing Passages

Anchor Standard	11th-12th Grade
CCRA.R.6	RL.11-12.1
	RL.11-12.4
CCRA.SL.1	SL.11-12.1

Objectives

- Students will cite strong and thorough textual evidence to support analysis of what the text says explicitly as well as inferences drawn from the text, including determining where the text leaves matters uncertain.
- Determine the meaning of words and phrases as they are used in the text, including figurative and connotative meanings; analyze the impact of specific word choices on meaning and tone, including words with multiple meanings or language that is particularly fresh, engaging, or beautiful.
- Analyze a case in which grasping a point of view requires distinguishing what is directly stated in a text from what is really meant (e.g., satire, sarcasm, irony, or understatement).
- Students will analyze the impact of specific word choices on meaning and tone.

Directions

On the pages that follow, there are 8 passages to analyze, each with a question or questions to guide the process. There are many ways to use these questions:

- You could use them as a worksheet for all students to complete individually.
- You could use the worksheet as your guide in a whole-class discussion. Have students turn to the first passage in the book, read it, and then ask the question(s) orally. Repeat through all 8 questions.
- You could assign one passage to each of 8 different groups of students, for the students to discuss and come up with responses to the question(s). Then hold a whole-class discussion.
- You could read the passage and then see which student can find the passage first (to practice skimming skills). Then follow up with the questions(s) and discussion.
- You could have students choose one or two questions to respond to in writing in their notebooks or journals.

Follow-Up/Assessment/Extension

- Ask students to gather passages that reveal information about Gatsby. How does the way that conflicting and withheld information help create a portrait of Gatsby?
- Have students write about the car accidents mentioned in the chapter. What causes accidents, according to Fitzgerald?
- Have students pick out other passages in this chapter that show interesting word usage, descriptions, or lack of clarity.
- As an introduction to this activity and this chapter, ask students to write about the responsibilities of being a good guest and a good host. What details from this chapter violate those social rules? What is the effect of this?

The Great Gatsby Chapter 3 Analyzing Passages

Answer the questions following the quotations completely.

1. "[Jordan's] gray, sun-strained eyes stared straight ahead, but she had deliberately shifted our relations, and for a moment I thought I loved her. But I am slow-thinking and full of interior rules that act as brakes on my desires, and I knew that first I had to get myself definitely out of that tangle back home. I'd been writing letters once a week and signing them: 'Love, Nick,' and all I could think of was how, when that certain girl played tennis, a faint mustache of perspiration appeared on her upper lip. Nevertheless there was a vague understanding that had to be tactfully broken off before I was free."

   What is Nick's "interior rule" here that "act[s] as brakes"?

2. "'See!' he cried triumphantly. 'It's a bona-fide piece of printed matter. It fooled me. This fella's a regular Belasco. It's a triumph. What thoroughness! What realism! Knew when to stop, too - didn't cut the pages. But what do you want? What do you expect?'"

   What does owning this possession say about Gatsby?

3. "I like to come," Lucille said. "I never care what I do, so I always have a good time. When I was here last I tore my gown on a chair, and he asked me my name and address – inside of a week I got a package from Croirier's with a new evening gown in it."

   "Did you keep it?" asked Jordan.

   "Sure I did. I was going to wear it tonight, but it was too big in the bust and had to be altered. It was gas blue with lavender beads. Two hundred and sixty-five dollars."

   What does the speaker's attitude toward her dress signify?

4. "He smiled understandingly—much more than understandingly. It was one of those rare smiles with a quality of eternal reassurance in it, that you may come across four or five times in life. It faced—or seemed to face—the whole external world for an instant, and then concentrated on you with an irresistible prejudice in your favor. It understood you just as far as you wanted to be understood, believed in you as you would like to believe in yourself, and assured you that it had precisely the impression of you that, at your best, you hoped to convey."

   Why the repetition of "understandingly"—what does the word mean in this context?

5. "It made no difference to me. Dishonesty in a woman is a thing you never blame deeply – I was casually sorry, and then I forgot. It was on that same house party that we had a curious conversation about driving a car. It started because she passed so close to some workmen that our fender flicked a button on one man's coat."

   What does this attitude reveal about Nick?

6. "'But how did it happen? Did you run into the wall?' 'Don't ask me,' said Owl Eyes, washing his hands of the whole matter. 'I know very little about driving — next to nothing. It happened, and that's all I know.'

   'Well, if you're a poor driver you oughtn't to try driving at night.'

   'But I wasn't even trying,' he explained indignantly, 'I wasn't even trying.'"

   How is the word "indignantly" significant here?

7. "Every one suspects himself of at least one of the cardinal virtues, and this is mine: I am one of the few honest people that I have ever known."

   Why is the word "suspects" significant?

8. "' At the enchanted metropolitan twilight I felt a haunting loneliness sometimes, and felt it in others – poor young clerks who loitered in front of windows waiting until it was time for a solitary restaurant dinner – young clerks in the dusk, wasting the most poignant moments of night and life."

   What is the effect of the city on Nick and others like him?

The Great Gatsby Chapter 3 Analyzing Passages Suggested Answers

Answer the questions following the quotations completely.

1. "[Jordan's] gray, sun-strained eyes stared straight ahead, but she had deliberately shifted our relations, and for a moment I thought I loved her. But I am slow-thinking and full of interior rules that act as brakes on my desires, and I knew that first I had to get myself definitely out of that tangle back home. I'd been writing letters once a week and signing them: 'Love, Nick,' and all I could think of was how, when that certain girl played tennis, a faint mustache of perspiration appeared on her upper lip. Nevertheless there was a vague understanding that had to be tactfully broken off before I was free."

   What is Nick's "interior rule" here that "act[s] as brakes"?
   Here Nick is conflicted over pursuing relationships with two different women. This is a question of honesty, which would likely be the "interior rule" that would be the "brakes"—the impetus to stop leading a woman on.

2. "'See!' he cried triumphantly. 'It's a bona-fide piece of printed matter. It fooled me. This fella's a regular Belasco. It's a triumph. What thoroughness! What realism! Knew when to stop, too - didn't cut the pages. But what do you want? What do you expect?'"

   What does owning this possession say about Gatsby?
   Gatsby has the resources to purchase an entire library of fine books, but the key detail here is that they have not yet been read. This suggests that Gatsby can acquire status symbols like books, but he does not have the benefit of the knowledge contained in them. The books are about appearance only, and nothing substantive.

3. "I like to come," Lucille said. "I never care what I do, so I always have a good time. When I was here last I tore my gown on a chair, and he asked me my name and address – inside of a week I got a package from Croirier's with a new evening gown in it."

   "Did you keep it?" asked Jordan.

   "Sure I did. I was going to wear it tonight, but it was too big in the bust and had to be altered. It was gas blue with lavender beads. Two hundred and sixty-five dollars."

   What does the speaker's attitude toward her dress signify?
   Her irresponsibility was rewarded—she ruined her own dress and Gatsby replaced it with a very expensive gown. She emphasizes the adornments and cost. This is a careless, wealthy, entitled person.

4. "He smiled understandingly—much more than understandingly. It was one of those rare smiles with a quality of eternal reassurance in it, that you may come across four or five times in life. It faced—or seemed to face—the whole external world for an instant, and then concentrated on you with an irresistible prejudice in your favor. It understood you just as far as you wanted to be understood, believed in you as you would like to believe in yourself, and assured you that it had precisely the impression of you that, at your best, you hoped to convey."

   Why the repetition of "understandingly"—what does the word mean in this context?
   "Understandingly" has dual meanings here, based on its denotation and connotation. Literally, "understandingly" means to comprehend. Its connotation suggests empathy, which is the state of feeling the same emotions as another person. This quality of Gatsby is a reflection of what he wants himself, being accepted by the world in the way he presents himself.

5. "It made no difference to me. Dishonesty in a woman is a thing you never blame deeply – I was casually sorry, and then I forgot. It was on that same house party that we had a curious conversation about driving a car. It started because she passed so close to some workmen that our fender flicked a button on one man's coat."

   What does this attitude reveal about Nick?
   This assertion calls into question Nick's claim that he does not judge people. Here he has different standards for men and women, and it can be perceived as patronizing.

6. "'But how did it happen? Did you run into the wall?' 'Don't ask me,' said Owl Eyes, washing his hands of the whole matter. 'I know very little about driving — next to nothing. It happened, and that's all I know.'

   Well, if you're a poor driver you oughtn't to try driving at night.'

   'But I wasn't even trying,' he explained indignantly, 'I wasn't even trying.'"

   How is the word "indignantly" significant here?
   To be indignant is to feel angry over a perceived injustice. Owl Eyes defends himself against the accusation of guilt for causing the accident. His defense, however, is that he "wasn't even trying," and acts like this excuse is legitimate enough to feel indignant over. Owl Eyes is revealed to be completely careless and reckless, with no semblance of rational thought or morality.

8. "Everyone suspects himself of at least one of the cardinal virtues, and this is mine: I am one of the few honest people that I have ever known."

   Why is the word "suspects" significant?
   To suspect is to believe in the truth of something, but it simultaneously means that the evidence is not fully credible. Nick makes a grand claim of being honest, but at the same time introduces doubt about it.

9. "' At the enchanted metropolitan twilight I felt a haunting loneliness sometimes, and felt it in others – poor young clerks who loitered in front of windows waiting until it was time for a solitary restaurant dinner – young clerks in the dusk, wasting the most poignant moments of night and life."

   What is the effect of the city on Nick and others like him?
   The effect of the city is a kind of isolation, turning inward even when there is a vital and busy world to engage in. It is a form of observation of life rather than participation in it.

The Great Gatsby Chapter 3

Reading Activity 3: Minor Characters

Anchor Standard	11th-12th Grade
CCRA.R.1	RL.11-12.1
CCRA.SL.1	SL.11-12.1

Objective

Using textual evidence, students will explore how minor characters, particularly those who are nearly caricatures, can create important meaning within the novel by offering a portrait of prevailing cultural mores.

Directions

The Minor Characters worksheet on the following page could be used in many ways, completed by small groups of students, individual students, or as a whole class activity.

Students can revisit this assignment later in the unit to compare how other minor characters are depicted and what their behaviors suggest about the times.

Students may (and should) use their books to skim through the chapters to refresh their memories or gather more information about the characters.

After students complete the worksheets discuss students' answers as a whole class. Collect the worksheets for grading, if you choose, or have students put them in their notebooks for further study.

Follow-Up/Assessment/Extension

Revisit this assignment later in the unit and compare the behaviors of Gatsby's party guests to those who attend the party that Tom and Daisy attend at Gatsby's house later in the novel. Do the behaviors remain the same, or do they change or intensify in some way?

The Great Gatsby Chapter 3 Reading Activity 3: Minor Characters

Complete the chart below using relevant quotes from the text that show how minor characters comported themselves at Gatsby's party. Then, after reviewing the quotes you selected, make observations about how the characters' behaviors reveal cultural mores (habits, manners, norms) of the times.

Character	Quote 1	Quote 2	Quote 3	Observations about cultural mores
Jordan's date				
Girls in yellow				
Owl Eyes				

The Great Gatsby Chapter 3
Reading Activity 3: Minor Characters Suggested Answers

Complete the chart below using relevant quotes from the text that show how minor characters comported themselves at Gatsby's party. Then, after reviewing the quotes you selected, make observations about how the characters' behaviors reveal cultural mores (habits, manners, norms) of the times.

Character	Quote 1	Quote 2	Quote 3	Observations about cultural mores
Jordan's date	"There were three married couples and Jordan's escort, a persistent undergraduate given to violent innuendo, and obviously under the impression that sooner or later Jordan was going to yield him up her person to a greater or lesser degree."	"Eluding Jordan's undergraduate, who was now engaged in an obstetrical conversation with two chorus girls, and who implored me to join him, I went inside."	"The undergraduate nodded in a cynical, melancholy way."	He is singly focused on the possibilities of finding someone for physical intimacy. He is rude and does not want to meet the host. Shows that some young men pursue sex.
Girls in yellow	"You don't know who we are," said one of the girls in yellow, "but we met you here about a month ago."	A pair of stage twins, who turned out to be the girls in yellow, did a baby act in costume, and champagne was served in glasses bigger than finger-bowls.	"I like to come," Lucille said. "I never care what I do, so I always have a good time. When I was here last I tore my gown on a chair, and he asked me my name and address — inside of a week I got a package from Croirier's with a new evening gown in it."	These are stereotypical "flappers" who seek out hedonism. They live like they are in a performance and as if there are no consequences. A "baby act" is apropos as they are immature and reckless.
Owl Eyes	"I was brought by a woman named Roosevelt," he continued. "Mrs. Claud Roosevelt. Do you know her? I met her somewhere last night. I've been drunk for about a week now, and I thought it might sober me up to sit in a library."	"But how did it happen? Did you run into the wall?" "Don't ask me," said Owl Eyes, washing his hands of the whole matter. "I know very little about driving — next to nothing. It happened, and that's all I know."	"I know nothing whatever about mechanics," he said decisively.	Owl Eyes is entitled and irresponsible. He feels a sense of propriety in having been brought to Gatsby's party, but remains a stranger to him. It is as if his position absolves him from responsibility—membership to a higher class affords him the right to be irresponsible.

The Great Gatsby Chapter 3

Reading Activity 4: Action, Character, Decision

Anchor Standard	11th-12th Grade
CCRA.R.1	RL.11-12.1
CCRA.SL.1	SL.11-12.1

Objective

Students will identify particular lines of dialogue or incidents in the story that propel the action, reveal aspects of character, or provoke a decision.

Directions

The following page contains passages from Chapter 3 of *The Great Gatsby*. Students should determine whether the passages advance the action, reveal aspects of a character, or provoke a decision.

This can be done as a whole-class activity, individually, or in small groups.

Follow-Up/Assessment/Extension

Have students skim Chapter 3 in the text to find one example of a passage that propels the action, one that reveals aspects of a character, and one that provokes a decision. Again, this could be done individually or as a group. This activity can be a quick prompt for starting class discussion of a reading assignment.

The Great Gatsby Chapter 3: Action, Character, Decision

Write **A** (for Action) **C** (for Character) or **D** (for Decision) in the blank next to each to identify whether the passage/statement advances the action, tells us more about a character, or provokes a decision. On the lines under each question, provide a short explanation of your choice.

___ 1. I was on my way to get roaring drunk from sheer embarrassment when Jordan Baker came out of the house and stood at the head of the marble steps, leaning a little backward and looking with contemptuous interest down into the garden.

___ 2. It was testimony to the romantic speculation he inspired that there were whispers about him from those who found little that it was necessary to whisper about in this world.

___ 3. We talked for a moment about some wet, gray little villages in France. Evidently he lived in this vicinity, for he told me that he had just bought a hydroplane, and was going to try it out in the morning.

___ 4. I wondered if the fact that he was not drinking helped to set him off from his guests, for it seemed to me that he grew more correct as the fraternal hilarity increased.

___ 5. But I am slow-thinking and full of interior rules that act as brakes on my desires, and I knew that first I had to get myself definitely out of that tangle back home.

The Great Gatsby Chapter 3:
Action, Character, Decision Suggested Answers

Write **A** (for Action) **C** (for Character) or **D** (for Decision) in the blank next to each to identify whether the passage/statement advances the action, tells us more about a character, or provokes a decision. On the lines under each question, provide a short explanation of your choice.

A 1. I was on my way to get roaring drunk from sheer embarrassment when Jordan Baker came out of the house and stood at the head of the marble steps, leaning a little backward and looking with contemptuous interest down into the garden.
Nick does not feel at ease at Gatsby's party, since it doesn't follow any of the polite social conventions that he is used to. Unable to greet the host, Nick drifts to the bar. The entire action of the book moves forward on Nick's meeting Jordan at the party, since it connects both Nick and Jordan to reuniting Gatsby and Daisy.

C 2. It was testimony to the romantic speculation he inspired that there were whispers about him from those who found little that it was necessary to whisper about in this world.
This passage speaks to the absolute "greatness" of Gatsby's character. Since so little is known about him, he has a "greatness" to be everything, a sum of all the gossip about him.

A 3. We talked for a moment about some wet, gray little villages in France. Evidently he lived in this vicinity, for he told me that he had just bought a hydroplane, and was going to try it out in the morning.
This is the moment—despite Nick's being unaware—that he has met Gatsby.

C 4. I wondered if the fact that he was not drinking helped to set him off from his guests, for it seemed to me that he grew more correct as the fraternal hilarity increased.
Nick observes Gatsby who is perfectly sober and extremely attentive in the midst of the drunken, hedonistic party he has thrown. Gatsby appears to be the opposite of his guests.

D 5. But I am slow-thinking and full of interior rules that act as brakes on my desires, and I knew that first I had to get myself definitely out of that tangle back home.
Nick, who believes himself to be honest, recognizes that before he more seriously pursues a relationship with Jordan, he must break off a relationship that he is currently in.

The Great Gatsby Chapter 3

Reading Activity 5: Figurative Language

Anchor Standard	11th-12th Grade
CCRA.R.4	RL.11-12.4
CCRA.SL.1	

Objectives

- Students will determine the meaning of words and phrases as they are used in the text, by examining similes and metaphors.
- Students will determine whether passages from the text are instances of simile or metaphor.

Directions

The following page has passages from the text that include similes and metaphors. This worksheet can be done individually, as a whole-class activity, or in small groups. Discuss the answers as a whole class. Collect the worksheets and record the grades if you choose to do so.

Follow-Up/Assessment/Extension

Ask students to annotate instances of these types of figurative language as they read. Consider whether any particular type is associated with particular characters.

The Great Gatsby Chapter 3: Figurative Language

On the short line provided, write S for simile, M for metaphor or N for neither. On the lines under each question, explain how the use of figurative language creates meaning.

___ 1. In his blue gardens men and girls came and went like moths among the whisperings and the champagne and the stars.

___ 2. By seven o'clock the orchestra has arrived, no thin five-piece affair, but a whole pitful of oboes and trombones and saxophones and viols and cornets and piccolos, and low and high drums.

___ 3. At least once a fortnight a corps of caterers came down with several hundred feet of canvas and enough colored lights to make a Christmas tree of Gatsby's enormous garden.

___ 4. A humorous suggestion was made that she sing the notes on her face, whereupon she threw up her hands, sank into a chair, and went off into a deep vinous sleep.

___ 5. ...at intervals she appeared suddenly at his side like an angry diamond, and hissed: "You promised!" into his ear.

___ 6. A wafer of a moon was shining over Gatsby's house, making the night fine as before, and surviving the laughter and the sound of his still glowing garden.

___ 7. Suddenly one of the gypsies, in trembling opal, seizes a cocktail out of the air, dumps it down for courage and, moving her hands like Frisco, dances out alone on the canvas platform.

___ 8. …but the girls had moved casually on and her remark was addressed to the premature moon, produced like the supper, no doubt, out of a caterer's basket.

___ 9. In the early morning the sun threw my shadow westward as I hurried down the white chasms of lower New York to the Probity Trust.

___ 10. …while his station wagon scampered like a brisk yellow bug to meet all trains.

The Great Gatsby Chapter 3: Figurative Language Suggested Answers

S 1. In his blue gardens men and girls came and went like moths among the whisperings and the champagne and the stars.
Here partygoers flit about and are compared to "Moths" using "like."

N 2. By seven o'clock the orchestra has arrived, no thin five-piece affair, but a whole pitful of oboes and trombones and saxophones and viols and cornets and piccolos, and low and high drums.
There is no use of simile or metaphor in the sentence.

M 3. At least once a fortnight a corps of caterers came down with several hundred feet of canvas and enough colored lights to make a Christmas tree of Gatsby's enormous garden.
The intimation of the comparison is that the garden is made as garish, colorful and bright as a Christmas tree.

M 4. A humorous suggestion was made that she sing the notes on her face, whereupon she threw up her hands, sank into a chair, and went off into a deep vinous sleep.
The direct comparison is music notes to the marks left by the crying woman's mascara on her cheeks.

S 5. ...at intervals she appeared suddenly at his side like an angry diamond, and hissed: "You promised!" into his ear.
The woman is compared to "an angry diamond," which suggests a snake (i.e. a diamondback), as it is followed by the word "hiss."

M 6. A wafer of a moon was shining over Gatsby's house, making the night fine as before, and surviving the laughter and the sound of his still glowing garden.
The comparison here is to a wafer, which usually means a thin slice of something, and may even refer to the Eucharist.

S 7. Suddenly one of the gypsies, in trembling opal, seizes a cocktail out of the air, dumps it down for courage and, moving her hands like Frisco, dances out alone on the canvas platform.
The partygoer is compared to a famous Vaudeville performer and dancer.

S 8. ...but the girls had moved casually on and her remark was addressed to the premature moon, produced like the supper, no doubt, out of a caterer's basket.
The moon is compared to the supper, which is described in fanciful, otherworldly terms.

N 9. In the early morning the sun threw my shadow westward as I hurried down the white chasms of lower New York to the Probity Trust.
No similes or metaphors are used here, though personification and synecdoche.

S 10. ...while his station wagon scampered like a brisk yellow bug to meet all trains.
The car is compared to an insect.

The Great Gatsby Chapter 3

Reading Activity 6: Elements of Fiction & Literary Devices

Anchor Standard	11th-12th Grade
CCRA.R.1	RL.11-12.1
	RL.11-12.2
	RL.11-12.4
	RL.11-12.5
CCRA.SL.1	SL.11-12.1

Objective

Students will study and discuss passages from the text to examine dialogue, hyperbole, foreshadowing, imagery, symbolism and suspense.

Directions

Use the following passages and discussion questions as a guide to discussing key elements of fiction and literary devices in this chapter. You can give students the questions ahead of time and have them formulate answers prior to the class discussion or you can jump right in with a whole class discussion without student preparation if your students will handle that well.

As you hold the class discussion, be sure to include conversations defining dialogue, hyperbole, foreshadowing, imagery, symbolism and suspense.

Follow-Up/Assessment/Extension

After your discussion, ask students to look for these elements in future chapters.

The Great Gatsby Chapter 3: Elements of Fiction & Literary Devices

1. The word yellow is used several times in the chapter. What is it primarily associated with?

2. How does Fitzgerald use hyperbole in describing Gatsby's party?

3. Car accidents are mentioned multiple times in this chapter. What is said about them?

4. Consider Nick and Jordan's conversation about car accidents. What might it foreshadow?

5. How does Fitzgerald create suspense around Gatsby's identity and personal history?

6. Compare Owl Eyes' dialogue in the library to his later dialogue at the scene of the car accident. Are they similar? Different? What does his diction suggest about him?

7. How does Gatsby's meeting with Jordan create suspense?

8. What is the "amputated wheel" a symbol of?

The Great Gatsby Chapter 3:
Elements of Fiction & Literary Devices Suggested Answers

1. **The word yellow is used several times in the chapter. What is it primarily associated with?**
The text mentions Gatsby's car as a "yellow bug," the orchestra plays "yellow cocktail music," and two guests who are professional show girls wear "twin yellow dresses." Yellow is a color associated with excess and conspicuous consumption.

2. **How does Fitzgerald use hyperbole in describing Gatsby's party?**
There are several examples, and the descriptions seem so outlandish that they seem hard to believe, but that is the point. The descriptions of citrus fruit, how long repairs after the party take, the size of champagne glasses. These are all examples of hyperbolic details.

3. **Car accidents are mentioned multiple times in this chapter. What is said about them?**
Owl Eyes has a car accident and draws a crowd of onlookers. Someone asks if he was trying to commit suicide. He is depicted as completely reckless. Nick and Jordan discuss car accidents and, as with Owl Eyes, Jordan declines to take responsibility.

4. **Consider Nick and Jordan's conversation about car accidents. What might it foreshadow?**
Jordan explains that she relies on other drivers to be careful. Nick challenges this idea: "Suppose you met somebody just as careless as yourself." This foreshadows the accident later in the book.

5. **How does Fitzgerald create suspense around Gatsby's identity and personal history?**
First by continually offering gossip about his background, then by having Jordan and Nick unsuccessfully looking for him, and finally to introduce him without introducing him at all.

6. **Compare Owl Eyes' dialogue in the library to his later dialogue at the scene of the car accident. Are they similar? Different? What does his diction suggest about him?**
He is impressed by the books being real—an appreciation for the showiness of such a library. He has no appreciation for the car he wrecks or the passenger in the car who could have been badly hurt. Both scenes are completely self-centered and self-absorbed.

7. **How does Gatsby's meeting with Jordan create suspense?**
First, she is mysteriously escorted away by the butler at Gatsby's request. After her meeting, she is exhilarated and begins to tell Nick about it, but then withholds due to her promise to Gatsby. This only makes the reader want to know more.

8. **What is the "amputated wheel" a symbol of?**
The wheel symbolizes waste caused by carelessness. The use of the word "amputated" is interesting because it personifies the wheel, as if the injury were human, and not just mechanical.

The Great Gatsby Chapter 3

Reading Activity 7: Meaning and Inferences

Anchor Standard	11th-12th Grade
CCRA.R.1	RL.11-12.1
CCRA.SL.1	SL.11-12.1

Objective

Students will answer questions about selected passages from the text which require them to extract meaning or inferences from the text.

Directions

The following pages contain passages from Chapter 3 of *The Great Gatsby* and questions related to the passages that require close reading to answer. Students should answer the questions related to the passages.

This can be done as a whole-class activity, individually, or in small groups. If it is done individually or in small groups, come together as a class to discuss the answers to the questions.

Follow-Up/Assessment/Extension

Collect the worksheets for review and/or grading. Ask students to keep these as possible raw material for writing essays in the future.

The Great Gatsby Chapter 3: Meaning & Inferences 1

Read the passages and answer the related questions.

1. I had been actually invited. A chauffeur in a uniform of robin's-egg blue crossed my lawn early that Saturday morning with a surprisingly formal note from his employer: the honor would be entirely Gatsby's, it said, if I would attend his "little party" that night. He had seen me several times, and had intended to call on me long before, but a peculiar combination of circumstances had prevented it — signed Jay Gatsby, in a majestic hand.

What in the passage conflicts with the idea of a "little party"?

2. As soon as I arrived I made an attempt to find my host, but the two or three people of whom I asked his whereabouts stared at me in such an amazed way, and denied so vehemently any knowledge of his movements, that I slunk off in the direction of the cocktail table — the only place in the garden where a single man could linger without looking purposeless and alone.

What do these reactions suggest that these people feel about Gatsby?

3. Instead of rambling, this party had preserved a dignified homogeneity, and assumed to itself the function of representing the staid nobility of the country-side — East Egg condescending to West Egg, and carefully on guard against its spectroscopic gayety.

What does this suggest about the party-goers' motives for attending the party?

4. Something in her tone reminded me of the other girl's "I think he killed a man," and had the effect of stimulating my curiosity. I would have accepted without question the information that Gatsby sprang from the swamps of Louisiana or from the lower East Side of New York. That was comprehensible. But young men didn't — at least in my provincial inexperience I believed they didn't — drift coolly out of nowhere and buy a palace on Long Island Sound.

What isn't "comprehensible" to Nick?

5. Jordan Baker instinctively avoided clever, shrewd men, and now I saw that this was because she felt safer on a plane where any divergence from a code would be thought impossible. She was incurably dishonest. She wasn't able to endure being at a disadvantage and, given this unwillingness, I suppose she had begun dealing in subterfuges when she was very young in order to keep that cool, insolent smile turned to the world and yet satisfy the demands of her hard, jaunty body.

What does this passage reveal about Jordan?

The Great Gatsby Chapter 3: Meaning & Inferences 1 Suggested Answers

1. I had been actually invited. A chauffeur in a uniform of robin's-egg blue crossed my lawn early that Saturday morning with a surprisingly formal note from his employer: the honor would be entirely Gatsby's, it said, if I would attend his "little party" that night. He had seen me several times, and had intended to call on me long before, but a peculiar combination of circumstances had prevented it — signed Jay Gatsby, in a majestic hand.

What in the passage conflicts with the idea of a "little party"?
The way that Gatsby uses "little party" shows how affected Gatsby is. The chauffeur and formal note give a very different impression than a casual or small get together.

2. As soon as I arrived I made an attempt to find my host, but the two or three people of whom I asked his whereabouts stared at me in such an amazed way, and denied so vehemently any knowledge of his movements, that I slunk off in the direction of the cocktail table — the only place in the garden where a single man could linger without looking purposeless and alone.

What do these reactions suggest that these people feel about Gatsby?
The guests' amazed stares suggest that everyone knows that no one ever really knows Gatsby or his whereabouts. They do not care about him, other than using him for his hospitality. They are willing to use him, but are content to remain ignorant about who he is as a person. They will gladly drink his liquor, eat his food, and destroy his property even though they don't really know him.

3. Instead of rambling, this party had preserved a dignified homogeneity, and assumed to itself the function of representing the staid nobility of the country-side — East Egg condescending to West Egg, and carefully on guard against its spectroscopic gayety.

What does this suggest about the party-goers' motives for attending the party?
This particular group of East Eggers kept to themselves. They want to take advantage of hospitality and nothing more; they are old money at a new money party.

4. Something in her tone reminded me of the other girl's "I think he killed a man," and had the effect of stimulating my curiosity. I would have accepted without question the information that Gatsby sprang from the swamps of Louisiana or from the lower East Side of New York. That was comprehensible. But young men didn't — at least in my provincial inexperience I believed they didn't — drift coolly out of nowhere and buy a palace on Long Island Sound.

What isn't "comprehensible" to Nick?
Nick is unable to understand how someone with an obscure biography and no apparent family connections could afford to purchase a home like Gatsby has. At least, with the limits of his "provincial experience" (growing up honest in the Midwest), Nick is unable to imagine how someone could rise up out of obscurity.

5. Jordan Baker instinctively avoided clever, shrewd men, and now I saw that this was because she felt safer on a plane where any divergence from a code would be thought impossible. She was incurably dishonest. She wasn't able to endure being at a disadvantage and, given this unwillingness, I suppose she had begun dealing in subterfuges when she was very young in order to keep that cool, insolent smile turned to the world and yet satisfy the demands of her hard, jaunty body.

What does this passage reveal about Jordan?
Jordan is concerned with her reputation and she is deeply competitive, and polite society provides her with a smoke screen to achieve those needs.

The Great Gatsby Chapter 3: Meaning & Inferences 2

Read the passage and answer the related questions.

"You're a rotten driver," I protested. "Either you ought to be more careful, or you oughtn't to drive at all."

"I am careful."

"No, you're not."

"Well, other people are," she said lightly.

"What's that got to do with it?"

"They'll keep out of my way," she insisted. "It takes two to make an accident."

"Suppose you met somebody just as careless as yourself."

"I hope I never will," she answered. "I hate careless people. That's why I like you."

1. How is Jordan being dishonest in this passage?

2. Is Nick being judgmental in this passage?

3. What causes an accident, according to Jordan? To Nick?

4. What does Jordan rely on to avoid accidents?

5. How is the whole passage a commentary on their relationship? Who is more of a hypocrite, Jordan or Nick?

The Great Gatsby Chapter 3: Meaning & Inferences 2 Suggested Answers

Read the passage and answer the related questions.

"You're a rotten driver," I protested. "Either you ought to be more careful, or you oughtn't to drive at all."

"I am careful."

"No, you're not."

"Well, other people are," she said lightly.

"What's that got to do with it?"

"They'll keep out of my way," she insisted. "It takes two to make an accident."

"Suppose you met somebody just as careless as yourself."

"I hope I never will," she answered. "I hate careless people. That's why I like you."

1. How is Jordan being dishonest in this passage?

She claims that she is "careful," but she knows that she is not.

2. Is Nick being judgmental in this passage?

He is; he calls Jordan on her lie, and then he does call her "careless."

3. What causes an accident, according to Jordan? To Nick?

According to Jordan, an accident is caused by two careless people. To Nick, only one careless person can cause an accident.

4. What does Jordan rely on to avoid accidents?
Jordan believes that other more responsible people prevent accidents.

5. How is the whole passage a commentary on their relationship? Who is more of a hypocrite, Jordan or Nick?
This passage could have a double meaning, the underlying one being the budding romance between the two. Reread the passage with that in mind. Nick is more of a hypocrite because he is seeing someone else currently. He is the careless party. Jordan hasn't proclaimed loyalty to anyone.

The Great Gatsby Chapter 3

Writing Activity 1: Who Is Gatsby?

Anchor Standard	9th-10th Grade
CCRA.SL.1	SL.11-12.1, 1a-1d
CCRA.SL.3	SL. 11-12.4
CCRA.W.1	W. 11-12.2
CCRA.W.2	W. 11-12.4
CCRA.W.4	W. 11-12.5
CCRA.W.5	W. 11-12.7
	W. 11-12.9, 9b

Objectives

- Students will evaluate and analyze textual evidence to determine who Gatsby is, and why Gatsby's character is revealed gradually.
- Students will evaluate passages about Gatsby to observe how he relates to emerging themes in the novel.
- Students will write a composition in which they consider their analysis of these interactions to answer the question, Who Is Gatsby?

Directions

The following series of worksheets and information organizers can be used by students individually, in small groups, or done partly as a whole-class activity. They are intended to guide students through the process of reading and thinking critically about information by ultimately answering the single question, "How do men relate to one another?"

Preview the following pages. Determine the best way to have your particular class handle this assignment (individually, pairs, groups, whole-class, or some combination). A combination of group work (to do the analyzing of the text on the chart page) followed by individual work (to do the second and third pages of the assignment) would most likely be best to fulfill the standards listed for this assignment.

Follow-Up/Assessment/Extension

- The written assignment will be a good basis for assessment of the students' success with this assignment. Create a rubric explaining the criteria on which their written assignments will be evaluated.
- Tell students to keep observing how Gatsby is presented, and if his biography is called into question.
- Have some students read/present their writing assignments to the class to practice more speaking/listening skills and to expose all students to each others' ideas.
- Use this assignment to introduce these themes: identity, reputation, and the American Dream.

The Great Gatsby Chapter 3: Who Is Gatsby?

In Chapter 3, after many allusions, the titular character, Jay Gatsby, is finally introduced to the reader. Yet, even after Gatsby is introduced, much about him remains vague.

For this assignment, you will identify passages about Gatsby as a way to form a clearer portrait of who he is and what rumors about him might be true.

To formulate an answer to the question "Who is Gatsby?":

1. Identify passages and quotes about Gatsby.

2. Examine the context of your quotes.

3. Consider the deeper meaning of the quotes:

    a. What is the tone of the speaker—friendly, adversarial, angry, competitive?
    b. Is the claim too exaggerated?
    c. Is there information inferred that is not wholly manifest?

4. Look for patterns in your evidence. Do multiple claims about Gatsby recur?

5. Decide what you believe is true about Gatsby.

The Great Gatsby Chapter 3: Who Is Gatsby?

Complete the chart to analyze information to develop ideas to write your essay.

Quote about or from Gatsby	Tone of the speaker?	Is the claim too exaggerated?	Is there information inferred that is not wholly manifest?

The Great Gatsby Chapter 3

Suggested Writing Assignments

Anchor Standard	11th-12th Grade
CCRA.W.1	W.11-12.1, 1a-1e
CCRA W.2	W.11-12.2, 2a-2f
CCRA.W.3	W.11-12.3, 3a-3e
CCRA.W.4	W.11-12.4
CCRA.W.5	W. 11-12.5

Objective

Students will be assigned or will choose one of a selection of writing assignments pertaining to Chapter 3 of *The Great Gatsby* to fulfill one or more of the standards listed above.

Directions

To provide you with maximum flexibility for differentiated instruction, the following page has a list of suggested writing assignments, all related to Chapter 3 of *The Great Gatsby*. Either assign individual students particular assignments to do or allow students to choose their own assignments.

A second page of "Quick Write" topics is also included.

Follow-Up/Assessment/Extension

- Have dramatic readings of students' narratives or poems.
- Create a "reading room" space in your classroom where students can donate their writing assignments for others in the class to read.
- Allow students to do more than one assignment if they want to.
- Use the "left-over" assignments (not chosen for this activity) as topics for journal entries.

The Great Gatsby Chapter 3: Creative Analytical Writing Assignments

1. Choose your favorite rumor about Gatsby and flesh it out into a whole absurd paragraph.
2. Write a scene with dialogue in which Jordan tells Nick precisely what she thinks of her date.
3. Write Owl Eyes' biography in a paragraph.
4. Write the script of the girls-in-yellows' "baby act." Make sure the content reflects the mores and attitudes of the partygoers.
5. Gatsby says that he is not a good host. Is that true?
6. Write a scene with dialogue of Gatsby talking to "Chicago" "on the wire."
7. Write a meta narrative of what Gatsby is thinking about during the moments as Tostoff's *Jazz History of the World* plays.
8. Write dialogue of Jordan's meeting with Gatsby.
9. Set aside Nick's claim to resist judging people. Write a paragraph from his perspective that honestly reflects how he feels about the people involved in the car accident.
10. Write a love letter from Jordan to Nick, enumerating reasons why she likes him.

The Great Gatsby Chapter 3: Quick-Write Writing Assignments

1. How are Jordan's date and Nick alike and/or different?

2. Describe the attitude of Gatsby's guests towards their host.

3. Compare Gatsby's behavior at his party to his guests' behavior. What does this reveal about Gatsby?

4. The story is set during Prohibition, yet alcohol is served at the party. What role does alcohol play in the chapter?

5. What is the significance of Owl Eyes? Does he have anything in common with T.J. Eckleburg?

6. What are some examples of carelessness in this chapter?

7. Gatsby is introduced through a series of rumors. What effect does this create in the narrative?

8. Why is the automobile wreck significant? What does it reveal about the people who attend Gatsby's parties?

9. Who is honest? Dishonest?

10. Nick describes his personal life/social life and relationship history. What does it reveal about him?

NOTES
THE GREAT GATSBY

MATERIALS: CHAPTERS 4-5
THE GREAT GATSBY

Reading Activity 1: True or False

Reading Activity 2: Analyzing Passages

Reading Activity 3: Foil Character Study

Reading Activity 4: Action, Character, Decision

Reading Activity 5: Figurative Language

Reading Activity 6: Elements of Fiction & Literary Devices

Reading Activity 7: Meaning and Inferences

Writing Activity 1: How Is Social Class Depicted?

Suggested Writing Assignments

Quick-Write Assignments

NOTES
THE GREAT GATSBY

The Great Gatsby Chapters 4-5

Reading Activity 1: True or False?

Anchor Standard	11th-12th Grade
CCRA.R.1	RL.11-12.1
CCRA.SL1	SL.11-12.1
CCRA SL.4	SL.11-12.4

Objectives

- Students will be able to cite the parts of the text that support their analysis of what the text says or infers.
- Students will consider statements about the text, determine whether those statements are true or false, and will give textual evidence supporting their choices.
- Students will work together in small groups to discuss, analyze, and evaluate the statements made.
- Students will evaluate the analytical work of their peers.

Directions

Prior to reading chapters 4-5: Give students (or post) the following list of statements about the chapters, and explain to students that they should read Chapters 4-5 to find out if these statements are true or false:

Gatsby is descended from a prominent Midwestern family.
Nick is offended by Gatsby's offer of employment.
Meyer Wolfsheim fixed the World's Series.
Jordan did not recognize Jay Gatsby when she met him in Long Island.
Daisy got drunk because she believed Gatsby was killed in the war.
Gatsby felt confident about reuniting with Daisy.

After reading Chapters 4-5: The worksheets on the following pages can be done by students individually, in small groups, or as a whole class. Below are directions to use the questions as a group activity to fulfill more state standards:

- Cut the worksheet apart, making each question and answer box a slip.
- Divide your class into six groups and give one question and a True/False evaluation form to each group. Tell students they are to discuss the statement and determine if the statement is true or false, supporting their decision with evidence from the text. Tell them their answers will be evaluated on the criteria given on the evaluation form.
- Give students ample time to discuss the statements and record their answers.
- Have the groups swap True or False question slips so that each group can evaluate another group's answer. The group should fill in the number of the question they are evaluating, decide how well the answer fulfills the criteria listed, and fill out the form accordingly.
- Repeat the previous step until all the groups have evaluated each others' answers.
- Collect the evaluations and answer slips.

The Great Gatsby Chapters 4-5: True or False?

Write *True* or *False* in the blank next to each statement. Below the statement, explain why you chose true or false, referencing the text to support your choices.

__________ 1. Gatsby is descended from a prominent Midwestern family.

__________ 2. Nick is offended by Gatsby's offer of employment.

__________ 3. Meyer Wolfsheim fixed the World's Series.

__________ 4. Jordan did not recognize Jay Gatsby when she met him in Long Island.

__________ 5. Daisy got drunk because she believed Gatsby was killed in the war.

__________ 6. Gatsby felt confident about reuniting with Daisy.

The Great Gatsby Chapters 4-5 True or False? Evaluation

List Your Group's Members: Your Group's Question # _______

___________________ ___________________ ___________________

___________________ ___________________ ___________________

1 = No, Not At All **2** = A Little **3** = Some **4** = Yes **5** = Yes, Very Well

Evaluation of Question # ___

Does the explanation support the answer of true or false? 1 2 3 4 5
Is there good textual evidence to support the answer? 1 2 3 4 5
Is the answer clearly stated? 1 2 3 4 5
Total Score ________ of a possible 15 points

Evaluation of Question # ___

Does the explanation support the answer of true or false? 1 2 3 4 5
Is there good textual evidence to support the answer? 1 2 3 4 5
Is the answer clearly stated? 1 2 3 4 5
Total Score ________ of a possible 15 points

Evaluation of Question # ___

Does the explanation support the answer of true or false? 1 2 3 4 5
Is there good textual evidence to support the answer? 1 2 3 4 5
Is the answer clearly stated? 1 2 3 4 5
Total Score ________ of a possible 15 points

Evaluation of Question # ___

Does the explanation support the answer of true or false? 1 2 3 4 5
Is there good textual evidence to support the answer? 1 2 3 4 5
Is the answer clearly stated? 1 2 3 4 5
Total Score ________ of a possible 15 points

Evaluation of Question # ___

Does the explanation support the answer of true or false? 1 2 3 4 5
Is there good textual evidence to support the answer? 1 2 3 4 5
Is the answer clearly stated? 1 2 3 4 5
Total Score ________ of a possible 15 points

The Great Gatsby Chapters 4-5: True or False? Suggested Answers

Write *True* or *False* in the blank next to each statement. Below the statement, explain why you chose true or false, referencing the text to support your choices.

FALSE 1. Gatsby is descended from a prominent Midwestern family.

Gatsby claims to be, but it is not true. When Nick asks him directly, he says he is from San Francisco, which is not in the Midwest.

TRUE 2. Nick is offended by Gatsby's offer of employment.

Nick is offended by Gatsby's offer. He feels that it is offered "in kind," "obviously and tactlessly" for services rendered, for reuniting Daisy and Jay. Nick makes an excuse that he is too busy for any "sidelines."

TRUE 3. Meyer Wolfsheim fixed the World's Series.

Nick is astonished by the audacity of the act: "The idea staggered me. I remembered of course that the World's Series had been fixed in 1919 but if I had thought of it at all I would have thought of it as a thing that merely HAPPENED, the end of some inevitable chain. It never occurred to me that one man could start to play with the faith of fifty million people--with the single-mindedness of a burglar blowing a safe."

TRUE 4. Jordan did not recognize Jay Gatsby when she met him in Long Island.

Though Jordan had met Gatsby when she was younger, she did not recognize him at his parties: "The officer looked at Daisy while she was speaking, in a way that every young girl wants to be looked at sometime, and because it seemed romantic to me I have remembered the incident ever since. His name was Jay Gatsby, and I didn't lay eyes on him again for over four years — even after I'd met him on Long Island I didn't realize it was the same man."

FALSE 5. Daisy got drunk because she believed Gatsby was killed in the war.

On the evening prior to her wedding day, Daisy gets drunk because she is conceivably still in love with Gatsby. She has a letter from him, but its contents are not disclosed.

FALSE 6. Gatsby felt confident about reuniting with Daisy.

Gatsby is intensely nervous prior to their meeting, and actually attempts to call it off at one point. His insecurity is seen in his gestures—having Nick's lawn mowed, sending flowers, feeling as if Nick has not provided proper refreshments.

The Great Gatsby Chapters 4-5
Reading Activity 2: Analyzing Passages

Anchor Standard	11th-12th Grade
CCRA.R.6	RL.11-12.1
	RL.11-12.4
CCRA.SL.1	SL.11-12.1

Objectives
- Students will cite strong and thorough textual evidence to support analysis of what the text says explicitly as well as inferences drawn from the text, including determining where the text leaves matters uncertain.
- Determine the meaning of words and phrases as they are used in the text, including figurative and connotative meanings; analyze the impact of specific word choices on meaning and tone, including words with multiple meanings or language that is particularly fresh, engaging, or beautiful.
- Analyze a case in which grasping a point of view requires distinguishing what is directly stated in a text from what is really meant (e.g., satire, sarcasm, irony, or understatement). Students will analyze the impact of specific word choices on meaning and tone.

Directions
On the pages that follow, there are 8 passages to analyze, each with a question or questions to guide the process. There are many ways to use these questions:

- You could use them as a worksheet for all students to complete individually.
- You could use the worksheet as your guide in a whole-class discussion. Have students turn to the first passage in the book, read it, and then ask the question(s) orally. Repeat through all 8 questions.
- You could assign one passage to each of 8 different groups of students, for the students to discuss and come up with responses to the question(s). Then hold a whole-class discussion.
- You could read the passage and then see which student can find the passage first (to practice skimming skills). Then follow up with the questions(s) and discussion.
- You could have students choose one or two questions to respond to in writing in their notebooks or journals.

Follow-Up/Assessment/Extension
- Ask students to gather passages that relate to Gatsby creating his identity and appearance.
- Have students write about the passage of time in the reunion scene.
- Have students pick out other passages in these chapters that show interesting word usage, descriptions, or lack of clarity.
- As an introduction to this activity and this chapters, ask students to write about the responsibilities of being a good guest and a good host. What details from this chapters violate those social rules? What is the effect of this?

The Great Gatsby Chapters 4-5 Analyzing Passages

Answer the questions following the quotations completely.

1. "He was balancing himself on the dashboard of his car with that resourcefulness of movement that is so peculiarly American — that comes, I suppose, with the absence of lifting work or rigid sitting in youth and, even more, with the formless grace of our nervous, sporadic games. This quality was continually breaking through his punctilious manner in the shape of restlessness. He was never quite still; there was always a tapping foot somewhere or the impatient opening and closing of a hand."

   Why is it significant that Gatsby always appears to be in motion?

2. "He looked at me sideways — and I knew why Jordan Baker had believed he was lying. He hurried the phrase "educated at Oxford," or swallowed it, or choked on it, as though it had bothered him before. And with this doubt, his whole statement fell to pieces, and I wondered if there wasn't something a little sinister about him, after all.

   'What part of the Middle West?' I inquired casually.

   'San Francisco.'"

   What is significant about Gatsby's answer?

3. "'Where've you been?' he demanded eagerly. 'Daisy's furious because you haven't called up.'
   'This is Mr. Gatsby, Mr. Buchanan.'
   They shook hands briefly, and a strained, unfamiliar look of embarrassment came over Gatsby's face.
   'How've you been, anyhow?' demanded Tom of me. 'How'd you happen to come up this far to eat?'
   'I've been having lunch with Mr. Gatsby.'
   I turned toward Mr. Gatsby, but he was no longer there."

   Why does Gatsby become embarrassed?

4. "I saw them in Santa Barbara when they came back, and I thought I'd never seen a girl so mad about her husband. If he left the room for a minute she'd look around uneasily, and say: 'Where's Tom gone?' and wear the most abstracted expression until she saw him coming in the door. She used to sit on the sand with his head in her lap by the hour, rubbing her fingers over his eyes and looking at him with unfathomable delight. It was touching to see them together — it made you laugh in a hushed, fascinated way. That was in August. A week after I left Santa Barbara Tom ran into a wagon on the Ventura road one night, and ripped a front wheel off his car. The girl who was with him got into the papers, too, because her arm was broken — she was one of the chambermaids in the Santa Barbara Hotel."

   What is Jordan missing about Daisy's behavior? Why is the repetition of Santa Barbara significant?

5. "'Yes.' His eyes went over it, every arched door and square tower. 'It took me just three years to earn the money that bought it.'

   'I thought you inherited your money.'

   'I did, old sport,' he said automatically, 'but I lost most of it in the big panic — the panic of the war.'

   I think he hardly knew what he was saying, for when I asked him what business he was in he answered, 'That's my affair,' before he realized that it wasn't the appropriate reply.

   'Oh, I've been in several things,' he corrected himself. 'I was in the drug business and then I was in the oil business. But I'm not in either one now.' He looked at me with more attention. 'Do you mean you've been thinking over what I proposed the other night?'"

   What does Gatsby misunderstand?

6. "He took out a pile of shirts and began throwing them, one by one, before us, shirts of sheer linen and thick silk and fine flannel, which lost their folds as they fell and covered the table in many-colored disarray. While we admired he brought more and the soft rich heap mounted higher — shirts with stripes and scrolls and plaids in coral and apple-green and lavender and faint orange, and monograms of Indian blue. Suddenly, with a strained sound, Daisy bent her head into the shirts and began to cry stormily.

   'They're such beautiful shirts,' she sobbed, her voice muffled in the thick folds. 'It makes me sad because I've never seen such — such beautiful shirts before.'"

   Why does Daisy cry?

7. "He hadn't once ceased looking at Daisy, and I think he revalued everything in his house according to the measure of response it drew from her well-loved eyes. Sometimes, too, he stared around at his possessions in a dazed way, as though in her actual and astounding presence none of it was any longer real. Once he nearly toppled down a flight of stairs. His bedroom was the simplest room of all — except where the dresser was garnished with a toilet set of pure dull gold. Daisy took the brush with delight, and smoothed her hair, whereupon Gatsby sat down and shaded his eyes and began to laugh."

   Why the emphasis on eyes?

8. "As I went over to say good-by I saw that the expression of bewilderment had come back into Gatsby's face, as though a faint doubt had occurred to him as to the quality of his present happiness. Almost five years! There must have been moments even that afternoon when Daisy tumbled short of his dreams — not through her own fault, but because of the colossal vitality of his illusion. It had gone beyond her, beyond everything. He had thrown himself into it with a creative passion, adding to it all the time, decking it out with every bright feather that drifted his way. No amount of fire or freshness can challenge what a man will store up in his ghostly heart."

   What has Gatsby "stored up?"

The Great Gatsby Chapters 4-5 Analyzing Passages Suggested Answers

Answer the questions following the quotations completely.

1. "He was balancing himself on the dashboard of his car with that resourcefulness of movement that is so peculiarly American — that comes, I suppose, with the absence of lifting work or rigid sitting in youth and, even more, with the formless grace of our nervous, sporadic games. This quality was continually breaking through his punctilious manner in the shape of restlessness. He was never quite still; there was always a tapping foot somewhere or the impatient opening and closing of a hand."

   Why is it significant that Gatsby always appears to be in motion?
   Gatsby is a consummate hustler, always on the make to better himself and his situation, a kind of personal manifest destiny. He is associated with his car and with his hydroplane, which are both about mobility and status. Gatsby continually seeks social mobility.

2. "He looked at me sideways — and I knew why Jordan Baker had believed he was lying. He hurried the phrase "educated at Oxford," or swallowed it, or choked on it, as though it had bothered him before. And with this doubt, his whole statement fell to pieces, and I wondered if there wasn't something a little sinister about him, after all.

   'What part of the Middle West?' I inquired casually.

   'San Francisco.'"

   What is significant about Gatsby's answer?
   San Francisco is not part of the Midwest, so this "wrong" answer confirms Nick's suspicions that Gatsby is neither honest nor forthright.

3. "'Where've you been?' he demanded eagerly. 'Daisy's furious because you haven't called up.'

   'This is Mr. Gatsby, Mr. Buchanan.'
   They shook hands briefly, and a strained, unfamiliar look of embarrassment came over Gatsby's face.
   'How've you been, anyhow?' demanded Tom of me. 'How'd you happen to come up this far to eat?'
   'I've been having lunch with Mr. Gatsby.'
   I turned toward Mr. Gatsby, but he was no longer there."

   Why does Gatsby become embarrassed?
   Tom's question about "com[ing] up this far to eat" literally makes Nick out of place. The same can be said for Gatsby, who is confronted by his romantic rival. "Strained" and "unfamiliar" are interesting because they suggest that Gatsby is unusually out of sorts, that he is confronted with a person and situation which he cannot control. Gatsby's response is to disappear.

4. "I saw them in Santa Barbara when they came back, and I thought I'd never seen a girl so mad about her husband. If he left the room for a minute she'd look around uneasily, and say: 'Where's Tom gone?' and wear the most abstracted expression until she saw him coming in the door. She used to sit on the sand with his head in her lap by the hour, rubbing her fingers over his eyes and looking at him with unfathomable delight. It was touching to see them together — it made you laugh in a hushed, fascinated way. That was in August. A week after I left Santa Barbara Tom ran into a wagon on the Ventura road one night, and ripped a front wheel off his car. The girl who was with him got into the papers, too, because her arm was broken — she was one of the chambermaids in the Santa Barbara Hotel."

   What is Jordan missing about Daisy's behavior? Why is the repetition of Santa Barbara significant?
   Daisy is being possessive of Tom, but for good reason, he is cheating on her. "Uneasily" and "abstracted" suggest Daisy's fear and mistrust. The second repetition of Santa Barbara, identifying the hotel where the woman worked, helps clarify the intimation that Tom was having affairs.

5. "'Yes.' His eyes went over it, every arched door and square tower. 'It took me just three years to earn the money that bought it.'

   'I thought you inherited your money.'

   'I did, old sport,' he said automatically, 'but I lost most of it in the big panic — the panic of the war.'

   I think he hardly knew what he was saying, for when I asked him what business he was in he answered, 'That's my affair,' before he realized that it wasn't the appropriate reply.

   'Oh, I've been in several things,' he corrected himself. 'I was in the drug business and then I was in the oil business. But I'm not in either one now.' He looked at me with more attention. 'Do you mean you've been thinking over what I proposed the other night?'"

   What does Gatsby misunderstand?
   Gatsby is unaware of why Nick inquired about his money—that Nick sees inconsistencies in Gatsby's personal history. Gatsby is also curt in his response, but realizes that Nick is perhaps different than most people he interacts with and requires a more thorough and polite answer. Nick is not interested in joining Gatsby in his illegal businesses.

6. "He took out a pile of shirts and began throwing them, one by one, before us, shirts of sheer linen and thick silk and fine flannel, which lost their folds as they fell and covered the table in many-colored disarray. While we admired he brought more and the soft rich heap mounted higher — shirts with stripes and scrolls and plaids in coral and apple-green and lavender and faint orange, and monograms of Indian blue. Suddenly, with a strained sound, Daisy bent her head into the shirts and began to cry stormily.

   'They're such beautiful shirts,' she sobbed, her voice muffled in the thick folds. 'It makes me sad because I've never seen such — such beautiful shirts before.'"

   Why does Daisy cry?
   Daisy is a wealthy woman, with a wealthy husband, who could have any shirts he wanted. Here Daisy is remorseful for the life she chose with Tom over a relationship with Gatsby, as she could have had very fine things with Gatsby, eventually, too.

7. "He hadn't once ceased looking at Daisy, and I think he revalued everything in his house according to the measure of response it drew from her well-loved eyes. Sometimes, too, he stared around at his possessions in a dazed way, as though in her actual and astounding presence none of it was any longer real. Once he nearly toppled down a flight of stairs. His bedroom was the simplest room of all — except where the dresser was garnished with a toilet set of pure dull gold. Daisy took the brush with delight, and smoothed her hair, whereupon Gatsby sat down and shaded his eyes and began to laugh."

   Why the emphasis on eyes?
   Eyes are all about seeing, in this case, Daisy seeing Gatsby's material possessions and Gatsby seeing Daisy (who is also perhaps a material possession). His bedroom has the least conspicuous consumption, except for the brush set. When Daisy takes the valuable item and uses it intimately (brushing her own hair), Gatsby is literally overcome, needing to shade his eyes.

8. "As I went over to say good-by I saw that the expression of bewilderment had come back into Gatsby's face, as though a faint doubt had occurred to him as to the quality of his present happiness. Almost five years! There must have been moments even that afternoon when Daisy tumbled short of his dreams — not through her own fault, but because of the colossal vitality of his illusion. It had gone beyond her, beyond everything. He had thrown himself into it with a creative passion, adding to it all the time, decking it out with every bright feather that drifted his way. No amount of fire or freshness can challenge what a man will store up in his ghostly heart."

   What has Gatsby "stored up?"
   Gatsby has "stored up" memories and an idealized vision of Daisy. The paradoxes "vitality of his illusion" and "ghostly heart" sum up Gatsby's interior life perfectly—the vision is more real than his reality.

The Great Gatsby Chapters 4-5

Reading Activity 3: Foil Character Study

Anchor Standard	11th-12th Grade
CCRA.R.1	RL.11-12.1
CCRA.SL.1	SL.11-12.1

Objective

Using textual evidence, students will explore how one relatively minor character can act as a foil to reveal more significant information about main characters.

Directions

The Foil Character Study worksheet on the following page could be used in many ways, completed by small groups of students, individual students, or as a whole class activity.

Students will be able to identify how details about a relatively minor character serve an additional function of revealing information about major characters.

Students may (and should) use their books to skim through the chapters to refresh their memories or gather more information about the characters.

After students complete the worksheets discuss students' answers as a whole class. Collect the worksheets for grading, if you choose, or have students put them in their notebooks for further study.

Follow-Up/Assessment/Extension

Revisit this assignment later in the unit and compare the way that Gatsby discusses Meyer Wolfsheim with the way he describes Dan Cody.

The Great Gatsby Chapters 4-5 Reading Activity 3: Foil Character Study

Complete the chart below with quotes from the text that describe Meyer Wolfsheim's interactions with Gatsby and Nick. Consider what these interactions reveal about Wolfsheim as well as about Gatsby and Nick.

Incident	Quotes/Phrases	What does this show about Gatsby?	What does this show about Nick?
Gatsby introducing Wolfsheim to Nick			
On opinions about the old Metropole			
On Gatsby going to Oxford			
On fixing the World's Series			

The Great Gatsby Chapters 4-5
Reading Activity 3: Foil Character Study Suggested Answers

Complete the chart below with quotes from the text that describe Meyer Wolfsheim's interactions with Gatsby and Nick. Consider what these interactions reveal about Wolfsheim as well as about Gatsby and Nick.

Incident	Quotes/Phrases	What does this show about Gatsby?	What does this show about Nick?
Gatsby introducing Wolfsheim to Nick	""…this is my friend Mr. Wolfsheim" "A small, flat-nosed Jew raised his large head and regarded me…"	Gatsby introduces Wolfsheim in a polite and formal way, as if their business is also polite and formal	Nick notices difference first—the primary detail being that Wolfsheim is Jewish. He makes his estimation of Wolfsheim based on appearance ("two fine growths of hair")
On opinions about the old Metropole	"Hot and small but full of memories" "Filled with friends gone now forever"	Gatsby specifically did not go to lunch there, though it sounds as if he and Wolfsheim are regulars there; too low-brow for Nick	Nick is aware of organized crime, but as a citizen aware of the news;he is entertained by Wolfsheim's stories.
On Gatsby going to Oxford	"He's an Oggsford man"	Gatsby's stories are easily digested by associates who are less cultured.	Nick is the narrator, so the spelling of Oggsford to illuminate the pronunciation is deliberate; hearing Wolfsheim laud Gatsby makes all Gatsby's claims less likely…perhaps this is showing Nick as judgmental.
On fixing the World's Series	"The idea staggered me…It never occurred to me that one man…"	Gatsby is in league with people who have accomplished staggering crimes; he is among the elite of organized crime	Nick has respect for an individual who has the gumption to act audaciously

The Great Gatsby Chapters 4-5

Reading Activity 4: Action, Character, Decision

Anchor Standard	11th-12th Grade
CCRA.R.1	RL.11-12.1
CCRA.SL.1	SL.11-12.1

Objective

Students will identify particular lines of dialogue or incidents in the story that propel the action, reveal aspects of character, or provoke a decision.

Directions

The following page contains passages from the Chapters 4-5 of *The Great Gatsby*. Students should determine whether the passages advance the action, reveal aspects of a character, or provoke a decision.

This can be done as a whole-class activity, individually, or in small groups.

Follow-Up/Assessment/Extension

Have students skim the Chapters 4-5 in the text to find one example of a passage that propels the action, one that reveals aspects of a character, and one that provokes a decision. Again, this could be done individually or as a group. This activity can be a quick prompt for starting class discussion of a reading assignment.

The Great Gatsby Chapters 4-5: Action, Character, Decision

Write **A** (for Action) **C** (for Character) or **D** (for Decision) in the blank next to each to identify whether the passage/statement advances the action, tells us more about a character, or provokes a decision. On the lines under each question, provide a short explanation of your choice.

___ 1. The officer looked at Daisy while she was speaking, in a way that every young girl wants to be looked at sometime, and because it seemed romantic to me I have remembered the incident ever since.

___ 2. Well, about six weeks ago, she heard the name Gatsby for the first time in years. It was when I asked you — do you remember? — if you knew Gatsby in West Egg. After you had gone home she came into my room and woke me up, and said: "What Gatsby?" and when I described him — I was half asleep — she said in the strangest voice that it must be the man she used to know. It wasn't until then that I connected this Gatsby with the officer in her white car.

___ 3. Gatsby, pale as death, with his hands plunged like weights in his coat pockets, was standing in a puddle of water glaring tragically into my eyes.

___ 4. They were sitting at either end of the couch, looking at each other as if some question had been asked, or was in the air, and every vestige of embarrassment was gone. Daisy's face was smeared with tears, and when I came in she jumped up and began wiping at it with her handkerchief before a mirror. But there was a change in Gatsby that was simply confounding. He literally glowed; without a word or a gesture of exultation a new well-being radiated from him and filled the little room..

___ 5. "Look at that," she whispered, and then after a moment: "I'd like to just get one of those pink clouds and put you in it and push you around."

___ 6. I think that voice held him most, with its fluctuating, feverish warmth, because it couldn't be over-dreamed — that voice was a deathless song..

The Great Gatsby Chapters 4-5:
Action, Character, Decision Suggested Answers

Write **A** (for Action) **C** (for Character) or **D** (for Decision) in the blank next to each to identify whether the passage/statement advances the action, tells us more about a character, or provokes a decision. On the lines under each question, provide a short explanation of your choice.

A 1. The officer looked at Daisy while she was speaking, in a way that every young girl wants to be looked at sometime, and because it seemed romantic to me I have remembered the incident ever since.

Jordan's ability to recollect Gatsby from the past leads to his reunion with Daisy, moving forward the action of the plot.

A 2. Well, about six weeks ago, she heard the name Gatsby for the first time in years. It was when I asked you — do you remember? — if you knew Gatsby in West Egg. After you had gone home she came into my room and woke me up, and said: "What Gatsby?" and when I described him — I was half asleep — she said in the strangest voice that it must be the man she used to know. It wasn't until then that I connected this Gatsby with the officer in her white car.

Jordan's casual mention of Gatsby caused Daisy to remember Gatsby and enquire if it was her lost love, moving forward the action of the plot.

C 3. Gatsby, pale as death, with his hands plunged like weights in his coat pockets, was standing in a puddle of water glaring tragically into my eyes.

Though seemingly urbane, powerful and wealthy, Gatsby is incredibly afraid and insecure when it comes to reuniting with Daisy.

D 4. They were sitting at either end of the couch, looking at each other as if some question had been asked, or was in the air, and every vestige of embarrassment was gone. Daisy's face was smeared with tears, and when I came in she jumped up and began wiping at it with her handkerchief before a mirror. But there was a change in Gatsby that was simply confounding. He literally glowed; without a word or a gesture of exultation a new well-being radiated from him and filled the little room.

The intimation is that they have expressed care and possibly love for each other, with an intention to pursue a relationship.

D 5. "Look at that," she whispered, and then after a moment: "I'd like to just get one of those pink clouds and put you in it and push you around."
Daisy is declaring her intentions—however fancifully—towards Gatsby, that she has romantic feelings for him.

C 6. I think that voice held him most, with its fluctuating, feverish warmth, because it couldn't be over-dreamed — that voice was a deathless song.
This is a statement on both Gatsby's and Daisy's character. He aspires to possess the "deathless song," and it is fundamental to who Daisy is—a sense of almost magical, romantic unreality.

The Great Gatsby Chapters 4-5

Reading Activity 5: Figurative Language

Anchor Standard	11th-12th Grade
CCRA.R.4	RL.11-12.4
CCRA.SL.1	

Objectives

- Students will determine the meaning of words and phrases as they are used in the text, by examining similes and metaphors.
- Students will determine whether passages from the text are instances of simile or metaphor.

Directions

The following page has passages from the text that include similes and metaphors.

This worksheet can be done individually, as a whole-class activity, or in small groups. Discuss the answers as a whole class. Collect the worksheets and record the grades if you choose to do so.

Follow-Up/Assessment/Extension

Ask students to annotate instances of these types of figurative language as they read. Consider whether any particular type is associated with particular characters.

The Great Gatsby Chapters 4-5: Figurative Language

On the short line provided, write S for simile, M for metaphor, or P for personification. On the lines under each question, explain how the use of figurative language creates meaning.

___ 1. It was a rich cream color, bright with nickel, swollen here and there in its monstrous length with triumphant hat-boxes and supper-boxes and tool-boxes, and terraced with a labyrinth of wind-shields that mirrored a dozen suns.

___ 2. With fenders spread like wings we scattered light through half Long Island City...

___ 3. It never occurred to me that one man could start to play with the faith of fifty million people — with the single-mindedness of a burglar blowing a safe.

___ 4. I had on a new plaid skirt also that blew a little in the wind, and whenever this happened the red, white, and blue banners in front of all the houses stretched out stiff and said tut-tut-tut-tut, in a disapproving way.

___ 5. I came into her room half an hour before the bridal dinner, and found her lying on her bed as lovely as the June night in her flowered dress — and as drunk as a monkey.

___ 6. She took it into the tub with her and squeezed it up into a wet ball, and only let me leave it in the soap-dish when she saw that it was coming to pieces like snow.

___ 7. At first I thought it was another party, a wild rout that had resolved itself into "hide-and-go-seek" or "sardines-in-the-box" with all the house thrown open to the game.

___ 8. The exhilarating ripple of her voice was a wild tonic in the rain.

___ 9. A damp streak of hair lay like a dash of blue paint across her cheek, and her hand was wet with glistening drops as I took it to help her from the car.

___ 10. As my taxi groaned away I saw Gatsby walking toward me across his lawn.

The Great Gatsby Chapters 4-5: Figurative Language Suggested Answers

On the short line provided, write S for simile, M for metaphor, or P for personification. On the lines under each question, explain how the use of figurative language creates meaning.

P 1. It was a rich cream color, bright with nickel, swollen here and there in its monstrous length with triumphant hat-boxes and supper-boxes and tool-boxes, and terraced with a labyrinth of wind-shields that mirrored a dozen suns.
Gatsby's car is described with the unusual adjective "swollen," which is not normally applied to cars, as they generally don't change size or shape in as dramatic a way.

S 2. With fenders spread like wings we scattered light through half Long Island City...
The comparison here is a car to a bird, using "like."

M 3. It never occurred to me that one man could start to play with the faith of fifty million people — with the single-mindedness of a burglar blowing a safe.
Here, given his criminal meddling with the World's Series, Nick compares Wolfsheim to a criminal that he imagines acts alone, a burglar robbing a safe.

P 4. I had on a new plaid skirt also that blew a little in the wind, and whenever this happened the red, white, and blue banners in front of all the houses stretched out stiff and said tut-tut-tut-tut, in a disapproving way.
In response to Jordan's skirt blowing a little provocatively, the banners—symbols of a staid, conservative community, voiced judgmental disapproval, a personification since banners do not talk.

S 5. I came into her room half an hour before the bridal dinner, and found her lying on her bed as lovely as the June night in her flowered dress — and as drunk as a monkey.
The comparison is direct, using "as," with an inebriated and out of control Daisy compared to a monkey.

S 6. She took it into the tub with her and squeezed it up into a wet ball, and only let me leave it in the soap-dish when she saw that it was coming to pieces like snow.
Gatsby's letter has disintegrated into pieces because it has gotten wet, and is compared here to snow, which is comprised of many small pieces.

M 7. At first I thought it was another party, a wild rout that had resolved itself into "hide-and-go-seek" or "sardines-in-the-box" with all the house thrown open to the game.
Nick compares Gatsby's parties to boisterous children's games.

M 8. The exhilarating ripple of her voice was a wild tonic in the rain.
A tonic is a drink that is meant to be restorative, almost medicinal, with an ability to cure ailments. Daisy's voice shares this restorative quality, at least for men.

S 9. A damp streak of hair lay like a dash of blue paint across her cheek, and her hand was wet with glistening drops as I took it to help her from the car.
Daisy's hair is compared to blue paint, which is an unusual comparison that foreshadows later events in the novel. The immediacy of the paint across her cheek is almost an urgent and violent image.

P 10. As my taxi groaned away I saw Gatsby walking toward me across his lawn.
Again, a car is given humanized characteristics, as cars generally do not groan.

The Great Gatsby Chapters 4-5

Reading Activity 6: Elements of Fiction & Literary Devices

Anchor Standard	11th-12th Grade
CCRA.R.1	RL.11-12.1
	RL.11-12.2
	RL.11-12.4
	RL.11-12.5
CCRA.SL.1	SL.11-12.1

Objective

Students will study and discuss passages from the text to examine flashback, suspense, conflict and plot.

Directions

Use the following passages and discussion questions as a guide to discussing key elements of fiction and literary devices in this chapters. You can give students the questions ahead of time and have them formulate answers prior to the class discussion or you can jump right in with a whole class discussion without student preparation if your students will handle that well.

As you hold the class discussion, be sure to include conversations defining flashback, suspense, conflict and plot.

Follow-Up/Assessment/Extension

After your discussion, ask students to look for these elements in future chapters.

The Great Gatsby Chapters 4-5: Elements of Fiction & Literary Devices

1. According to Jordan, what happened in October 1917?

2. The flashback to 1917 occurs somewhat abruptly in the middle of Chapter 4, between Nick's lunch with Gatsby and a romantic encounter with Jordan. Is there significance to this juxtaposition?

3. The flashback is recounted from Nick's recollection of hearing the story from Jordan. Why is this choice of perspective significant?

4. Nick's thought, "There are only the pursued, the pursuing, the busy, and the tired." How does this relate to the flashback and Gatsby's scheme, which Jordan is revealing to Nick?

5. Consider the temporal aspects of the plot. What is the primary conflict in Chapters 4 and 5?

6. How does Fitzgerald use the concept of waiting to build suspense in Chapters 4 and 5?

7. In these chapters, characters are not given all the information available in a linear way. Which characters is information withheld from? Why?

The Great Gatsby Chapters 4-5: Elements of Fiction & Literary Devices Suggested Answers

1. According to Jordan, what happened in October 1917?
   Daisy was 18 years old and was very popular among the officers from Camp Taylor for dates. Daisy called Jordan over to her car to ask that she tell the volunteers at the Red Cross that she would not be coming in. Jordan recalled Gatsby, specifically the way he looked at Daisy.

2. The flashback to 1917 occurs somewhat abruptly in the middle of Chapter 4, between Nick's encounter with Wolfsheim and Gatsby and a romantic encounter with Jordan. Is there significance to this juxtaposition?
   Gatsby knows that Nick is scheduled to meet Jordan for tea, and Gatsby becomes the architect of Nick's entire day, driving him to the city and having lunch together, then allowing Jordan to explain the details of his plan for reuniting with Daisy and to ask for Nick's assistance on his behalf. Nick goes on about the way that Meyer Wolfsheim affected so many people by manipulating the outcome of the World's Series, much like the way Gatsby is manipulating the outcome of a relationship with Daisy.

3. The flashback is recounted from Nick's recollection of hearing the story from Jordan. Why is this choice of perspective significant?
   While an omniscient narrator would provide more detail, hearing the story through Jordan allows for important omissions. For example, she knows that Gatsby and Daisy were talking in the white roadster, but she does not know what they were saying. By recounting the story to Nick and sharing her attitudes ("Daisy ought to have something in her life."), it creates another way to frame and understand Jordan and Nick's relationship, which bookends Chapter 4.

4. Nick's thought, "There are only the pursued, the pursuing, the busy, and the tired." How does this relate to the flashback and Gatsby's scheme, which Jordan is revealing to Nick?
   It is skeptical, and in that sense, connects Nick's attitude to Jordan's ("wan," "cynical," "scornful") and speaks to how people are manipulators or manipulated.

5. Consider the temporal aspects of the plot. What is the primary conflict in Chapters 4 and 5?
   The primary conflict is man versus time; can Gatsby overcome the past and recover the affections of the woman he values so dearly.

6. How does Fitzgerald use the concept of waiting to build suspense in Chapters 4 and 5?
   Nick must wait to get filled in on Gatsby's plan by Jordan. The beginning of Chapter 5 focuses on Nick and Gatsby waiting for Daisy, with Gatsby's anxiety increasing to the point when he actually calls off the meeting.

7. In these chapters, characters are not given all the information available in a linear way. Which characters is information withheld from? Why?
   Information is withheld from Nick by Jordan (at Gatsby's request) and Gatsby, so as not to offend him if he was friendly with Tom. Information is withheld from Daisy by Nick, Jordan and Gatsby, to make the reunion with Gatsby appear spontaneous rather than an elaborate years-long manipulation.

The Great Gatsby Chapters 4-5

Reading Activity 7: Meaning and Inferences

Anchor Standard	11th-12th Grade
CCRA.R.1	RL.11-12.1
CCRA.SL.1	SL.11-12.1

Objective

Students will answer questions about selected passages from the text which require them to extract meaning or inferences from the text.

Directions

The following pages contain passages from Chapters 4-5 of *The Great Gatsby* and questions related to the passages that require close reading to answer. Students should answer the questions related to the passages.

This can be done as a whole-class activity, individually, or in small groups. If it is done individually or in small groups, come together as a class to discuss the answers to the questions.

Follow-Up/Assessment/Extension

Collect the worksheets for review and/or grading. Ask students to keep these as possible raw material for writing essays in the future.

The Great Gatsby Chapters 4-5: Meaning & Inferences 1

Read the passages and answer the related questions.

1. From East Egg, then, came the Chester Beckers and the Leeches, and a man named Bunsen, whom I knew at Yale, and Doctor Webster Civet, who was drowned last summer up in Maine. And the Hornbeams and the Willie Voltaires, and a whole clan named Blackbuck, who always gathered in a corner and flipped up their noses like goats at whosoever came near. And the Ismays and the Chrysties (or rather Hubert Auerbach and Mr. Chrystie's wife), and Edgar Beaver, whose hair, they say, turned cotton-white one winter afternoon for no good reason at all.

Clarence Endive was from East Egg, as I remember. He came only once, in white knicker-bockers, and had a fight with a bum named Etty in the garden. From farther out on the Island came the Cheadles and the O. R. P. Schraeders, and the Stonewall Jackson Abrams of Georgia, and the Fishguards and the Ripley Snells. Snell was there three days before he went to the penitentiary, so drunk out on the gravel drive that Mrs. Ulysses Swett's automobile ran over his right hand. The Dancies came, too, and S. B. Whitebait, who was well over sixty, and Maurice A. Flink, and the Hammerheads, and Beluga the tobacco importer, and Beluga's girls.

What is the significance of the list of names?

2. "It was a photograph of half a dozen young men in blazers loafing in an archway through which were visible a host of spires. There was Gatsby, looking a little, not much, younger — with a cricket bat in his hand.

Then it was all true. I saw the skins of tigers flaming in his palace on the Grand Canal; I saw him opening a chest of rubies to ease, with their crimson-lighted depths, the gnawings of his broken heart."

Why does Nick change his mind about Gatsby?

3. “We passed a barrier of dark trees, and then the facade of Fifty-ninth Street, a block of delicate pale light, beamed down into the park. Unlike Gatsby and Tom Buchanan, I had no girl whose disembodied face floated along the dark cornices and blinding signs, and so I drew up the girl beside me, tightening my arms. Her wan, scornful mouth smiled, and so I drew her up again closer, this time to my face.”

How does Nick feel about Jordan?

4. "...They were sitting at either end of the couch looking at each other as if some question had been asked or was in the air, and every vestige of embarrassment was gone. Daisy's face was smeared with tears and when I came in she jumped up and began wiping at it with her handkerchief before a mirror. But there was a change in Gatsby that was simply confounding. He literally glowed; without a word or a gesture of exultation a new well-being radiated from him and filled the little room."

What “question” has likely been asked?

5. "If it wasn't for the mist we could see your home across the bay... You always have a green light that burns all night at the end of your dock."

What is the significance of the proximity and of the mist obscuring the view?

The Great Gatsby Chapters 4-5:
Meaning & Inferences 1 Suggested Answers

1. From East Egg, then, came the Chester Beckers and the Leeches, and a man named Bunsen, whom I knew at Yale, and Doctor Webster Civet, who was drowned last summer up in Maine. And the Hornbeams and the Willie Voltaires, and a whole clan named Blackbuck, who always gathered in a corner and flipped up their noses like goats at whosoever came near. And the Ismays and the Chrysties (or rather Hubert Auerbach and Mr. Chrystie's wife), and Edgar Beaver, whose hair, they say, turned cotton-white one winter afternoon for no good reason at all.

Clarence Endive was from East Egg, as I remember. He came only once, in white knickerbockers, and had a fight with a bum named Etty in the garden. From farther out on the Island came the Cheadles and the O. R. P. Schraeders, and the Stonewall Jackson Abrams of Georgia, and the Fishguards and the Ripley Snells. Snell was there three days before he went to the penitentiary, so drunk out on the gravel drive that Mrs. Ulysses Swett's automobile ran over his right hand. The Dancies came, too, and S. B. Whitebait, who was well over sixty, and Maurice A. Flink, and the Hammerheads, and Beluga the tobacco importer, and Beluga's girls.

What is the significance of the list of names?
Here Nick goes to the effort to know guests by name, particularly because he feels these guests slight Gatsby by not caring who he is and commercing in rumors about him. Look at the names: Cheadles (cheat), Schraeders (shredders), Fishguards (guarder of fish), Snells (snell is a part of a fishing line), Swett (sweat), Dancies (suggesting flitty), Flink (fink), Hammerheads (shark) & Beluga (a fish). None of these names is flattering. They all have negative connotations when associated with a person.

2. "It was a photograph of half a dozen young men in blazers loafing in an archway through which were visible a host of spires. There was Gatsby, looking a little, not much, younger — with a cricket bat in his hand.

Then it was all true. I saw the skins of tigers flaming in his palace on the Grand Canal; I saw him opening a chest of rubies to ease, with their crimson-lighted depths, the gnawings of his broken heart."

Why does Nick change his mind about Gatsby?
Gatsby has already shown Nick "proof" of his identity in the form of mementos like the medal he was awarded. Nick actually stifles his laughter and finds Gatsby's claims to be not very credible. Seeing the photo changes Nick's opinion, not for any rational reason, but because he sees Gatsby in this context and feels empathy for the way that Gatsby's romantic dreams were crushed. From the photo, Nick can imagine Gatsby in the situations—no matter how far-fetched they seem—that he described.

3. “We passed a barrier of dark trees, and then the facade of Fifty-ninth Street, a block of delicate pale light, beamed down into the park. Unlike Gatsby and Tom Buchanan, I had no girl whose disembodied face floated along the dark cornices and blinding signs, and so I drew up the girl beside me, tightening my arms. Her wan, scornful mouth smiled, and so I drew her up again closer, this time to my face.”

How does Nick feel about Jordan?
He loves the one he’s with—he is not enamored with or possessed by any woman, so Jordan will do because she is there.

4. "...They were sitting at either end of the couch looking at each other as if some question had been asked or was in the air, and every vestige of embarrassment was gone. Daisy's face was smeared with tears and when I came in she jumped up and began wiping at it with her handkerchief before a mirror. But there was a change in Gatsby that was simply confounding. He literally glowed; without a word or a gesture of exultation a new well-being radiated from him and filled the little room."

What “question” has likely been asked?
They likely discuss the status of their feelings toward one another, as well as Daisy’s feelings toward Gatsby when she decided to marry to Tom. Daisy felt regret; Gatsby got the answer he desired.

5. "If it wasn't for the mist we could see your home across the bay... You always have a green light that burns all night at the end of your dock."

What is the significance of the proximity and of the mist obscuring the view?
Gatsby can get close to Daisy, but he will be separated from her, by a natural boundary like a bay or by social status. He literally cannot see her house in through the mist, but has an abiding belief that it is there and that she is waiting to be acquired by him, with a green light (like a green traffic light) beckoning him forward.

The Great Gatsby Chapters 4-5: Meaning & Inferences 2

Read the passage and answer the related questions.

Gatsby, his hands still in his pockets, was reclining against the mantelpiece in a strained counterfeit of perfect ease, even of boredom. His head leaned back so far that it rested against the face of a defunct mantelpiece clock, and from this position his distraught eyes stared down at Daisy, who was sitting, frightened but graceful, on the edge of a stiff chair.

"We've met before," muttered Gatsby. His eyes glanced momentarily at me, and his lips parted with an abortive attempt at a laugh. Luckily the clock took this moment to tilt dangerously at the pressure of his head, whereupon he turned and caught it with trembling fingers, and set it back in place. Then he sat down, rigidly, his elbow on the arm of the sofa and his chin in his hand.

"I'm sorry about the clock," he said.

My own face had now assumed a deep tropical burn. I couldn't muster up a single commonplace out of the thousand in my head.

"It's an old clock," I told them idiotically.

I think we all believed for a moment that it had smashed in pieces on the floor.

"We haven't met for many years," said Daisy, her voice as matter-of-fact as it could ever be.

"Five years next November."

1. Why is the word "counterfeit" significant?

2. Why is the word "defunct" significant?

3. Why do they believe that the clock broke?

4. What is this scene actually about?

5. Compare Gatsby and Daisy's behavior in the passage.

The Great Gatsby Chapters 4-5: Meaning & Inferences 2 Suggested Answers

Gatsby, his hands still in his pockets, was reclining against the mantelpiece in a strained counterfeit of perfect ease, even of boredom. His head leaned back so far that it rested against the face of a defunct mantelpiece clock, and from this position his distraught eyes stared down at Daisy, who was sitting, frightened but graceful, on the edge of a stiff chair.

"We've met before," muttered Gatsby. His eyes glanced momentarily at me, and his lips parted with an abortive attempt at a laugh. Luckily the clock took this moment to tilt dangerously at the pressure of his head, whereupon he turned and caught it with trembling fingers, and set it back in place. Then he sat down, rigidly, his elbow on the arm of the sofa and his chin in his hand.

"I'm sorry about the clock," he said.

My own face had now assumed a deep tropical burn. I couldn't muster up a single commonplace out of the thousand in my head.

"It's an old clock," I told them idiotically.

I think we all believed for a moment that it had smashed in pieces on the floor.

"We haven't met for many years," said Daisy, her voice as matter-of-fact as it could ever be.

"Five years next November."

1. Why is the word "counterfeit" significant?
Here it is supposed to describe Gatsby's affect, his attempt to be calm though he is nervous. It serves to describe Gatsby thoroughly, as his whole life is counterfeit.

2. Why is the word "defunct" significant?
The clock is literally stopped, just as Gatsby seeks to arrest time and pretend that five years have not gone by. "Defunct," however, is a negatively connoted word.

3. Why do they believe that the clock broke?
The way that Gatsby is acting so intensely, his grave and serious response suggests that the clock actually broke.

4. What is this scene actually about?
The scene is about how fragile time is—can Gatsby be successful trying to rekindle the past.

5. Compare Gatsby and Daisy's behavior in the passage.
Gatsby is nervous and highly focused, while Daisy is emotional and matter-of-fact.

The Great Gatsby Chapters 4-5

Writing Activity 1: How Is Social Class Depicted?

Anchor Standard	11th-12th Grade
CCRA.SL.1	SL.11-12.1, 1a-1d
CCRA.SL.3	SL. 11-12.4
CCRA.W.1	W. 11-12.2
CCRA.W.2	W. 11-12.4
CCRA.W.4	W. 11-12.5
CCRA.W.5	W. 11-12.7
	W. 11-12.9, 9b

Objectives

- Students will evaluate and analyze textual evidence to determine what the novel suggests about the role of social class in America.
- Students will evaluate passages about social class to develop ideas about this major theme in the novel.
- Students will write a composition in which they consider their analysis of these passages to answer the question, How Is Social Class Depicted?

Directions

The following series of worksheets and information organizers can be used by students individually, in small groups, or done partly as a whole-class activity. They are intended to guide students through the process of reading and thinking critically about information by ultimately answering the single question, "How is social class depicted in the novel?

Preview the following pages. Determine the best way to have your particular class handle this assignment (individually, pairs, groups, whole-class, or some combination). A combination of group work (to do the analyzing of the text on the chart page) followed by individual work (to do the second and third pages of the assignment) would most likely be best to fulfill the standards listed for this assignment.

Follow-Up/Assessment/Extension

- The written assignment will be a good basis for assessment of the students' success with this assignment. Create a rubric explaining the criteria on which their written assignments will be evaluated.
- Tell students to keep observing how members of different social classes in the novel are depicted.
- Have some students read/present their writing assignments to the class to practice more speaking/listening skills and to expose all students to each others' ideas.
- Use this assignment to introduce these themes: class, wealth, power, social mobility and the American Dream.

The Great Gatsby Chapters 4-5: How Is Social Class Depicted in the Novel?

In Chapters 4-5, many parallels are drawn between Gatsby and a British aristocrat. Fitzgerald is making a commentary on the role of money in society, putting both Nick and the reader in the position of observer of Gatsby's ostentatious show of wealth.

For this assignment, you will identify passages about Gatsby and his wealth, as well as Nick's reflections on his observations, as a way to understand what Fitzgerald is suggesting about money and the upper tier of society who enjoys access to very large sums of money.

To determine an idea about how social class is depicted in the novel:

1. Identify passages and quotes about Gatsby's wealth, especially any references to British aristocracy.

2. Examine the context of your quotes.

3. Consider the deeper meaning of the quotes:

    a. What is the tone—is it positive or negative?
    b. Is the quote advocating for the lifestyle Gatsby lives or cautioning against it?
    c. How do others view Gatsby's wealth?

4. Look for patterns in your evidence. Do multiple opinions about Gatsby's wealth recur?

5. Decide what statement you believe the text is making about social class.

The Great Gatsby Chapters 4-5: How Is Social Class Depicted?

Complete the chart to analyze information to develop ideas to write your essay.

Quote about Gatsby's wealth	Tone: positive or negative?	Does the idea advocate for or caution against Gatsby's lifestyle and class ambition?	How do others view Gatsby's wealth in this passage?

The Great Gatsby Chapters 4-5

Suggested Writing Assignments

Anchor Standard	11th-12th Grade
CCRA.W.1	W.11-12.1, 1a-1e
CCRA W.2	W.11-12.2, 2a-2f
CCRA.W.3	W.11-12.3, 3a-3e
CCRA.W.4	W.11-12.4
CCRA.W.5	W. 11-12.5

Objective

Students will be assigned or will choose one of a selection of writing assignments pertaining to Chapters 4-5 of *The Great Gatsby* to fulfill one or more of the standards listed above.

Directions

To provide you with maximum flexibility for differentiated instruction, the following page has a list of suggested writing assignments, all related to Chapters 4-5 of *The Great Gatsby*. Either assign individual students particular assignments to do or allow students to choose their own assignments.

A second page of "Quick Write" topics is also included.

Follow-Up/Assessment/Extension

- Have dramatic readings of students' narratives or poems.
- Create a "reading room" space in your classroom where students can donate their writing assignments for others in the class to read.
- Allow students to do more than one assignment if they want to.
- Use the "left-over" assignments (not chosen for this activity) as topics for journal entries.

The Great Gatsby Chapters 4-5: Creative Analytical Writing Assignments

1. Write the backstory of Meyer Wolfsheim.
2. Choose one of the stories that Gatsby shares about his past (rubies, Oxford, etc.) and write it out.
3. Write Klipspringer's biography in a paragraph.
4. Describe how Gatsby's car suits him; describe how Daisy's roadster suits her.
5. Write the obituary of the person in the funeral procession.
6. Write a diary entry from Jordan's perspective about why she looked up to Daisy.
7. Write a stream-of-consciousness paragraph of what Daisy thinks when she first sees Gatsby.
8. Imagine Gatsby created a room in the house for Daisy. Describe its contents.
9. Write a poem about the mist and the green light.
10. Write a thank you note from Gatsby to Jordan, thanking her for making the connection to Daisy that he has sought for so long.

The Great Gatsby Chapters 4-5: Quick-Write Writing Assignments

1. What additional details about the place are added as Gatsby and Nick drive through the valley of ashes?
2. In what ways was Daisy disobedient as a girl?
3. What does Jordan think about coincidences?
4. What about Jordan does Nick find attractive?
5. How is Gatsby an actor? Does the "real Gatsby" ever emerge?
6. How does the green light symbolize the American Dream?
7. Is Nick a hypocrite for essentially helping Daisy start an affair, when he did not relish his time with Tom and Myrtle?
8. Can Daisy live up to Gatsby's expectations?
9. What role does love play in a marriage? In an affair?
10. Why is Gatsby reluctant to allow Nick to leave?

MATERIALS: CHAPTERS 6-7
THE GREAT GATSBY

Reading Activity 1: True or False

Reading Activity 2: Analyzing Passages

Reading Activity 3: Static and Dynamic Characters

Reading Activity 4: Action, Character, Decision

Reading Activity 5: Figurative Language

Reading Activity 6: Elements of Fiction & Literary Devices

Reading Activity 7: Meaning and Inferences

Writing Activity 1: Moral Failure In The Great Gatsby

Suggested Writing Assignments

Quick-Write Assignments

NOTES
THE GREAT GATSBY

The Great Gatsby Chapters 6-7

Reading Activity 1: True or False?

Anchor Standard	11th-12th Grade
CCRA.R.1	RL.11-12.1
CCRA.SL1	SL.11-12.1
CCRA SL.4	SL.11-12.4

Objectives

- Students will be able to cite the parts of the text that support their analysis of what the text says or infers.
- Students will consider statements about the text, determine whether those statements are true or false, and will give textual evidence supporting their choices.
- Students will work together in small groups to discuss, analyze, and evaluate the statements made.
- Students will evaluate the analytical work of their peers.

Directions

Prior to reading Chapters 6-7: Give students (or post) the following list of statements about the chapters, and explain to students that they should read Chapters 6-7 to find out if these statements are true or false:

Gatsby hires organized crime acquaintances to act as domestic servants because of their discretion.
The cause of Wilson's illness is learning that his wife was having an extramarital affair.
Gatsby's wealth was mainly inherited from Dan Cody.
Tom purchased a big, new yellow car.
Daisy claims that she never loved Tom at all.
Tom hits Daisy and breaks her nose when he learns that she drove the death car.

After reading Chapters 6-7: The worksheets on the following pages can be done by students individually, in small groups, or as a whole class. Below are directions to use the questions as a group activity to fulfill more state standards:

- Cut the worksheet apart, making each question and answer box a slip.
- Divide your class into six groups and give one question and a True/False evaluation form to each group. Tell students they are to discuss the statement and determine if the statement is true or false, supporting their decision with evidence from the text. Tell them their answers will be evaluated on the criteria given on the evaluation form.
- Give students ample time to discuss the statements and record their answers.
- Have the groups swap True or False question slips so that each group can evaluate another group's answer. The group should fill in the number of the question they are evaluating, decide how well the answer fulfills the criteria listed, and fill out the form accordingly.
- Repeat the previous step until all the groups have evaluated each others' answers.
- Collect the evaluations and answer slips.

The Great Gatsby Chapters 6-7: True or False?

Write *True* or *False* in the blank next to each statement. Below the statement, explain why you chose true or false, referencing the text to support your choices.

__________ 1. Gatsby hires organized crime acquaintances to act as domestic servant because of their discretion.

__________ 2. The cause of Wilson's illness is learning that his wife was having an extramarital affair.

__________ 3. Gatsby's wealth was mainly inherited from Dan Cody.

__________ 4. Tom purchased a big, new yellow car.

__________ 5. Daisy claims that she never loved Tom at all.

__________ 6. Tom hits Daisy and breaks her nose when he learns that she drove the death car.

The Great Gatsby Chapters 6-7 True or False? Evaluation

List Your Group's Members: Your Group's Question # _______

___________________ ___________________ ___________________

___________________ ___________________ ___________________

1 = No, Not At All **2** = A Little **3** = Some **4** = Yes **5** = Yes, Very Well

Evaluation of Question # ___
Does the explanation support the answer of true or false? 1 2 3 4 5
Is there good textual evidence to support the answer? 1 2 3 4 5
Is the answer clearly stated? 1 2 3 4 5
Total Score ________ of a possible 15 points

Evaluation of Question # ___
Does the explanation support the answer of true or false? 1 2 3 4 5
Is there good textual evidence to support the answer? 1 2 3 4 5
Is the answer clearly stated? 1 2 3 4 5
Total Score ________ of a possible 15 points

Evaluation of Question # ___
Does the explanation support the answer of true or false? 1 2 3 4 5
Is there good textual evidence to support the answer? 1 2 3 4 5
Is the answer clearly stated? 1 2 3 4 5
Total Score ________ of a possible 15 points

Evaluation of Question # ___
Does the explanation support the answer of true or false? 1 2 3 4 5
Is there good textual evidence to support the answer? 1 2 3 4 5
Is the answer clearly stated? 1 2 3 4 5
Total Score ________ of a possible 15 points

Evaluation of Question # ___
Does the explanation support the answer of true or false? 1 2 3 4 5
Is there good textual evidence to support the answer? 1 2 3 4 5
Is the answer clearly stated? 1 2 3 4 5
Total Score ________ of a possible 15 points

The Great Gatsby Chapters 6-7: True or False? Suggested Answers

Write *True* or *False* in the blank next to each statement. Below the statement, explain why you chose true or false, referencing the text to support your choices.

TRUE 1. Gatsby hires organized crime acquaintances to act as domestic servants because of their discretion.

True, as the "general opinion in the village was that the new people weren't servants at all." Gatsby wanted to avoid gossip about Daisy "com[ing] over quite often."

TRUE 2. The cause of Wilson's illness is learning that his wife was having an extramarital affair.

When Tom inquires about Wilson's ailment, Wilson responds that he is "all run down." Nick, however, recognizes the "parallel discovery" that the men share, that their wives are romantically involved with other men.

FALSE 3. Gatsby's wealth was mainly inherited from Dan Cody.

Though Dan Cody was a millionaire and Gatsby was to inherit $25,000, he received none of it due to a "legal device that was used against him." The result was that the "remaining millions went intact to Ella Kaye."

FALSE 4. Tom purchased a big, new yellow car.

Tom is driving Gatsby's car, or as he calls it, a "circus wagon." While taunting Wilson about the sale of his blue coupe, Tom claims that he had purchased this new car. Ultimately this fabrication leads to Myrtle's death.

FALSE 5. Daisy claims that she never loved Tom at all.

Daisy rejects this claim, which Gatsby pressures her to make: "Just tell him the truth—that you never loved him—and it's all wiped out forever." Daisy declines and says Gatsby "want[s] too much." Tom also rejects this claim, and appeals to Daisy to confirm that she loved him.

FALSE 6. Tom hits Daisy and breaks her nose when he learns that she drove the death car.

Though a concerned Gatsby stands "vigil" outside of the Buchanan home for fear of reprisals from Tom if he should learn the truth about who was ultimately responsible for Myrtle's death, Tom and Daisy can be seen in the kitchen, with "an unmistakable air of natural intimacy about the picture, and anybody would have said that they were conspiring together."

The Great Gatsby Chapters 6-7

Reading Activity 2: Analyzing Passages

Anchor Standard	11th-12th Grade
CCRA.R.6	RL.11-12.1
	RL.11-12.4
CCRA.SL.1	SL.11-12.1

Objectives

- Students will cite strong and thorough textual evidence to support analysis of what the text says explicitly as well as inferences drawn from the text, including determining where the text leaves matters uncertain.
- Determine the meaning of words and phrases as they are used in the text, including figurative and connotative meanings; analyze the impact of specific word choices on meaning and tone, including words with multiple meanings or language that is particularly fresh, engaging, or beautiful.
- Analyze a case in which grasping a point of view requires distinguishing what is directly stated in a text from what is really meant (e.g., satire, sarcasm, irony, or understatement).
- Students will analyze the impact of specific word choices on meaning and tone.

Directions

On the pages that follow, there are 8 passages to analyze, each with a question or questions to guide the process. There are many ways to use these questions:

- You could use them as a worksheet for all students to complete individually.
- You could use the worksheet as your guide in a whole-class discussion. Have students turn to the first passage in the book, read it, and then ask the question(s) orally. Repeat through all 8 questions.
- You could assign one passage to each of 8 different groups of students, for the students to discuss and come up with responses to the question(s). Then hold a whole-class discussion.
- You could read the passage and then see which student can find the passage first (to practice skimming skills). Then follow up with the questions(s) and discussion.
- You could have students choose one or two questions to respond to in writing in their notebooks or journals.

Follow-Up/Assessment/Extension

- Ask students to gather passages that relate to the influences of Dan Code on Gatsby.
- Have students write about the descriptions of the main characters who attend Gatsby's party, particularly Tom and Daisy.
- Have students pick out other passages in this chapters that show interesting word usage, descriptions, or lack of clarity.
- As an introduction to this activity and these chapters, ask students to write about relationships, and if affairs are ever justified. Ask students to examine characters' attitudes about this topic.

The Great Gatsby Chapters 6-7 Analyzing Passages

Answer the questions following the quotations completely.

1. "I suppose he'd had the name ready for a long time, even then. His parents were shiftless and unsuccessful farm people — his imagination had never really accepted them as his parents at all. The truth was that Jay Gatsby of West Egg, Long Island, sprang from his Platonic conception of himself. He was a son of God — a phrase which, if it means anything, means just that — and he must be about His Father's business, the service of a vast, vulgar, and meretricious beauty. So he invented just the sort of Jay Gatsby that a seventeen-year-old boy would be likely to invent, and to this conception he was faithful to the end."

   The word meretricious means relating to prostitution. What does this usage suggest about Gatsby?

2. "'She has a big dinner party and he won't know a soul there.' He frowned. 'I wonder where in the devil he met Daisy. By God, I may be old-fashioned in my ideas, but women run around too much these days to suit me. They meet all kinds of crazy fish.'"

   Why is this ironic?

3. "It was like that. Almost the last thing I remember was standing with Daisy and watching the moving-picture director and his Star. They were still under the white plum tree and their faces were touching except for a pale, thin ray of moonlight between. It occurred to me that he had been very slowly bending toward her all evening to attain this proximity, and even while I watched I saw him stoop one ultimate degree and kiss at her cheek."

   Why is this significant?

4. "Her glance left me and sought the lighted top of the steps, where *Three O'clock in the Morning*, a neat, sad little waltz of that year, was drifting out the open door. After all, in the very casualness of Gatsby's party there were romantic possibilities totally absent from her world. What was it up there in the song that seemed to be calling her back inside? What would happen now in the dim, incalculable hours? Perhaps some unbelievable guest would arrive, a person infinitely rare and to be marveled at, some authentically radiant young girl who with one fresh glance at Gatsby, one moment of magical encounter, would blot out those five years of unwavering devotion."

   What does this suggest about Daisy's state of mind?

5. "His heart beat faster and faster as Daisy's white face came up to his own. He knew that when he kissed this girl, and forever wed his unutterable visions to her perishable breath, his mind would never romp again like the mind of God. So he waited, listening for a moment longer to the tuning-fork that had been struck upon a star. Then he kissed her. At his lips' touch she blossomed for him like a flower and the incarnation was complete."

   What is the "incarnation" here? How does Gatsby change?

6. "'She's got an indiscreet voice,' I remarked. 'It's full of ——' I hesitated.'
   'Her voice is full of money,' he said suddenly.
   That was it. I'd never understood before. It was full of money — that was the inexhaustible charm that rose and fell in it, the jingle of it, the cymbals' song of it. . . . high in a white palace the king's daughter, the golden girl. . ."

   What does this suggest about Daisy? About the way Gatsby views her?

7. "The relentless beating heat was beginning to confuse me and I had a bad moment there before I realized that so far his suspicions hadn't alighted on Tom. He had discovered that Myrtle had some sort of life apart from him in another world, and the shock had made him physically sick. I stared at him and then at Tom, who had made a parallel discovery less than an hour before — and it occurred to me that there was no difference between men, in intelligence or race, so profound as the difference between the sick and the well. Wilson was so sick that he looked guilty, unforgivably guilty — as if he had just got some poor girl with child."

   What is the relationship between "sick" and "guilty" here?

8. "Michaelis and this man reached her first, but when they had torn open her shirtwaist, still damp with perspiration, they saw that her left breast was swinging loose like a flap, and there was no need to listen for the heart beneath. The mouth was wide open and ripped at the corners, as though she had choked a little in giving up the tremendous vitality she had stored for so long."

   What does the contrast between her violent death and her life (as Nick imagines it) suggest about Myrtle?

The Great Gatsby Chapters 6-7
Analyzing Passages Suggested Answers

Answer the questions following the quotations completely.

1. "I suppose he'd had the name ready for a long time, even then. His parents were shiftless and unsuccessful farm people — his imagination had never really accepted them as his parents at all. The truth was that Jay Gatsby of West Egg, Long Island, sprang from his Platonic conception of himself. He was a son of God — a phrase which, if it means anything, means just that — and he must be about His Father's business, the service of a vast, vulgar, and meretricious beauty. So he invented just the sort of Jay Gatsby that a seventeen-year-old boy would be likely to invent, and to this conception he was faithful to the end."

   The word "meretricious" means relating to prostitution. What does this usage suggest about Gatsby?
   The use of the word suggests that a monetary value is related to the essence of Gatsby, even to his very "conception," and that it is his birthright and destiny to promote a materialistic worldview. "Beauty" here is "meretricious," which means nothing is beautiful and admired merely for beauty's sake, but that everything is viewed as a commodity with an associated value. The belief of this is so strongly ingrained in Gatsby that it is like his religion, with capitalism being his personal god.

2. "'She has a big dinner party and he won't know a soul there.' He frowned. 'I wonder where in the devil he met Daisy. By God, I may be old-fashioned in my ideas, but women run around too much these days to suit me. They meet all kinds of crazy fish.'"

   Why is this ironic?
   In this passage, Tom observes that Gatsby does not accurately observe social cues of the upper class, and is judging him for it and emphasizing that—despite his wealth—Gatsby would be an outsider ("he won't know a soul..."). Tom has arrived at the Gatsby's home unannounced and unexpected, as the guest of a woman who barely knows Gatsby, which makes the horse-riding party somewhat rude guests. Tom also refers to Daisy socializing with Gatsby in an informal way, which is precisely what he is doing. Tom's "old-fashioned" "ideas" must not extend to his own mistress (Myrtle), who does indeed "run around" to be with Tom.

3. "It was like that. Almost the last thing I remember was standing with Daisy and watching the moving-picture director and his Star. They were still under the white plum tree and their faces were touching except for a pale, thin ray of moonlight between. It occurred to me that he had been very slowly bending toward her all evening to attain this proximity, and even while I watched I saw him stoop one ultimate degree and kiss at her cheek."

   Fitzgerald sketches out this image, devoting over a paragraph to this nameless Hollywood couple. Why?
   The couple is like Daisy and Gatsby—a highly comprised romance story is played out where Nick can observe it. The constant movement of the man towards the woman ("proximity") is like Gatsby putting himself in physical (across the bay) and social (throwing his lavish parties) "proximity" to Daisy, with her romantic affections as the prize for his efforts.

4. "Her glance left me and sought the lighted top of the steps, where *Three O'clock in the Morning*, a neat, sad little waltz of that year, was drifting out the open door. After all, in the very casualness of Gatsby's party there were romantic possibilities totally absent from her world. What was it up there in the song that seemed to be calling her back inside? What would happen now in the dim, incalculable hours? Perhaps some unbelievable guest would arrive, a person infinitely rare and to be marvelled at, some authentically radiant young girl who with one fresh glance at Gatsby, one moment of magical encounter, would blot out those five years of unwavering devotion."

   What does this suggest about Daisy's state of mind?
   Daisy likes being the object of Gatsby's affection. "Those five years of unwavering devotion" are from Gatsby to Daisy. "Unwavering" is not an apt description for her, as she married Tom, even if she felt love for Gatsby. The narrator imagines Daisy imagining that she could be supplanted by someone "rare" and "to be marveled at," both indicators of value, which Gatsby might want to possess. A threat to her perceived value in Gatsby's eyes is what makes her most reluctant to leave.

5. "His heart beat faster and faster as Daisy's white face came up to his own. He knew that when he kissed this girl, and forever wed his unutterable visions to her perishable breath, his mind would never romp again like the mind of God. So he waited, listening for a moment longer to the tuning-fork that had been struck upon a star. Then he kissed her. At his lips' touch she blossomed for him like a flower and the incarnation was complete."

   What is the "incarnation" here? How does Gatsby change?
   As Gatsby kisses Daisy, he feels as though he is now married to her ("forever wed") because of his intentions to change and become someone else entirely, someone with wealth and power and access to Daisy's social class. This is the "incarnation," as Gatsby's intentions turn him into someone else.

6. "'She's got an indiscreet voice,' I remarked. 'It's full of ——' I hesitated.'
   'Her voice is full of money,' he said suddenly.
   That was it. I'd never understood before. It was full of money — that was the inexhaustible charm that rose and fell in it, the jingle of it, the cymbals' song of it. . . . high in a white palace the king's daughter, the golden girl. . ."

   What does this suggest about Daisy? About the way Gatsby views her?
   The comparison of Daisy's voice to money suggests that Gatsby sees her as a possession more than as a person. It also suggests that her words have the power of currency—they can get her the things she wants. The comparison further suggests that this quality is the basis of her allure—it and her position ("high in a white palace the king's daughter…")—not any depth of character, goodness or intellect.

7. "The relentless beating heat was beginning to confuse me and I had a bad moment there before I realized that so far his suspicions hadn't alighted on Tom. He had discovered that Myrtle had some sort of life apart from him in another world, and the shock had made him physically sick. I stared at him and then at Tom, who had made a parallel discovery less than an hour before — and it occurred to me that there was no difference between men, in intelligence or race, so profound as the difference between the sick and the well. Wilson was so sick that he looked guilty, unforgivably guilty — as if he had just got some poor girl with child."

   What is the relationship between "sick" and "guilty" here?
   What is interesting is that Nick is comparing Tom and Wilson, who both recently learned of their wives' infidelities. The description is a paradox—one might assume that Tom would feel sick, yet he is comparatively "well." To further the paradox, Wilson is so "sick" that he seems "guilty," so "guilty" that it is as if he engaged in sexual relations and gotten "some poor girl" pregnant. This suggests that the "sickness" is moral in nature—Wilson is terribly affected by his discovery, yet the amoral Tom is "well."

8. "Michaelis and this man reached her first, but when they had torn open her shirtwaist, still damp with perspiration, they saw that her left breast was swinging loose like a flap, and there was no need to listen for the heart beneath. The mouth was wide open and ripped at the corners, as though she had choked a little in giving up the tremendous vitality she had stored for so long."

   What does the contrast between her violent death and her life (as Nick imagines it) suggest about Myrtle?
   Her "tremendous vitality" had been "stored for so long," which is not how the other more carefree, reckless characters comport themselves—they indulge in affairs and parties and other excesses. Here the brutal violence of her death seems proportional to the kind of sensuous, passionate life that she aspired to live (with Tom), the "breast" and "heart," which sustained gruesome damage, both being associated with sexual and romantic intimacy.

The Great Gatsby Chapters 6-7

Reading Activity 3: Static and Dynamic Characters

Anchor Standard	11th-12th Grade
CCRA.R.1	RL.11-12.1
CCRA.SL.1	SL.11-12.1

Objectives

- Using textual evidence, students will explore how characters are static and dynamic.
- Students will be able to identify which characters in chapters 6-7 are static or dynamic.
- Students can use their current observations about the characters' growth or absence of growth.
- Students will think about how plot influences characters and how characters' changes (or lack of changes) contribute to meaning in the novel.

Directions

The static and dynamic character worksheet on the following page could be used in many ways, completed by small groups of students, individual students, or as a whole class activity.

After students complete the worksheets discuss students' answers as a whole class. Collect the worksheets for grading, if you choose, or have students put them in their notebooks for further study.

Follow-Up/Assessment/Extension

Revisit this assignment later in the unit and discuss the relationship between characters' change and the novel's major themes in small groups or as a whole class.

The Great Gatsby Chapters 6-7
Reading Activity 3: Static and Dynamic Characters

A character can be either dynamic or static. A dynamic character grows or progresses in some way as plot in a story moves forward. A static character does not undergo a change and stays fundamentally the same.

From the list of characters below, put the names of two dynamic characters in the relevant boxes and names of two static characters in the relevant boxes. Complete the chart, using actual quotes when asked and noting page numbers. Use your book to locate relevant passages. Note: whether or not some characters are dynamic or static can be debatable; be sure to use compelling textual evidence to support your claims.

Jordan | Nick | Gatsby | Daisy | Tom | Myrtle | Wilson

Dynamic Character	Quote – Observation 1 (Find a quote that shows how a character was before changing. Write the quote below.)	Quote – Observation 2 (Find a quote that shows how a character has undergone change. Write the quote below.)	Describe the Character's Change
Name of Static Character	Quote – Observation 1 (Find a quote that describes a quality or attitude of a static character. Write the quote below.)	Quote – Observation 2 (Find a quote later in the novel that shows that the character has the same quality or attitude. Write the quote below.)	Describe the Character's Quality or Attitude

The Great Gatsby Chapters 6-7
Static and Dynamic Characters Suggested Answers

Jordan | Nick | Gatsby | Daisy | Tom | Myrtle | Wilson

Name of Dynamic Character	Quote – Observation 1 (Find a quote that shows how a character was before changing. Write the quote below.)	Quote – Observation 2 (Find a quote that shows how a character has undergone change. Write the quote below.)	Describe the Character's Change
Name of Static Character	**Quote – Observation 1 (Find a quote that describes a quality or attitude of a static character. Write the quote below.)**	**Quote – Observation 2 (Find a quote later in the novel that shows that the character has the same quality or attitude. Write the quote below.)**	**Describe the Character's Quality or Attitude**

Exact passages chosen will vary, but students' work should show these things about the characters:

Jordan is primarily a static character; in these chapters she remains silent about her involvement in aiding Daisy's affair with Gatsby. She continues to be aloof and mostly ambivalent.

If the reader believes Nick's claims at the beginning of the novel that he is honest and refrains from judging others, Nick is largely a static character. He shows his growing disdain for Tom in these chapters, as well as a deepening awareness that Gatsby cannot repeat the past.

As a character, Gatsby remains the same, and is steadfastly focused on attaining Daisy.

Daisy is temporarily emboldened by her affair with Gatsby, flouting it in front of Tom. She also openly taunts Tom about his affairs at Gatsby's party.

Tom continues to be reckless and judgmental, especially of Gatsby.

Myrtle resists against being confined by her husband and is desperate to avoid moving away. She risks and loses her life to this end.

Wilson undergoes change by becoming "sick," or being affected by the world's immortality. He goes from not noticing his wife to being centrally focused on her. He also conducts his business with more urgency.

The Great Gatsby Chapters 6-7

Reading Activity 4: Action, Character, Decision

Anchor Standard	11th-12th Grade
CCRA.R.1	RL.11-12.1
CCRA.SL.1	SL.11-12.1

Objective

Students will identify particular lines of dialogue or incidents in the story that propel the action, reveal aspects of character, or provoke a decision.

Directions

The following page contains passages from the Chapters 6-7 of *The Great Gatsby*. Students should determine whether the passages advance the action, reveal aspects of a character, or provoke a decision.
This can be done as a whole-class activity, individually, or in small groups.

Follow-Up/Assessment/Extension

Have students skim the Chapters 6-7 in the text to find one example of a passage that propels the action, one that reveals aspects of a character, and one that provokes a decision.

Again, this could be done individually or as a group. This activity can be a quick prompt for starting class discussion of a reading assignment.

The Great Gatsby Chapters 6-7: Action, Character, Decision

Write **A** (for Action) **C** (for Character) or **D** (for Decision) in the blank next to each to identify whether the passage/statement advances the action, tells us more about a character, or provokes a decision. On the lines under each question, provide a short explanation of your choice.

___ 1. James Gatz — that was really, or at least legally, his name. He had changed it at the age of seventeen and at the specific moment that witnessed the beginning of his career — when he saw Dan Cody's yacht drop anchor over the most insidious flat on Lake Superior.

___ 2. It was indirectly due to Cody that Gatsby drank so little. Sometimes in the course of gay parties women used to rub champagne into his hair; for himself he formed the habit of letting liquor alone.

___ 3. "Who is this Gatsby anyhow?" demanded Tom suddenly. "Some big bootlegger?"

___ 4. "I wanted somebody who wouldn't gossip. Daisy comes over quite often — in the afternoons."

___ 5. "'You two start on home, Daisy,' said Tom. 'In Mr. Gatsby's car.'
She looked at Tom, alarmed now, but he insisted with magnanimous scorn."

___ 6. "The God damned coward!" he whimpered. "He didn't even stop his car."

The Great Gatsby Chapters6-7:
Action, Character, Decision Suggested Answers

Write **A** (for Action) **C** (for Character) or **D** (for Decision) in the blank next to each to identify whether the passage/statement advances the action, tells us more about a character, or provokes a decision. On the lines under each question, provide a short explanation of your choice.

D 1. James Gatz — that was really, or at least legally, his name. He had changed it at the age of seventeen and at the specific moment that witnessed the beginning of his career — when he saw Dan Cody's yacht drop anchor over the most insidious flat on Lake Superior.
Young Gatsby seizes an opportunity to provide a valuable and heroic service to someone unlike him—wealthy. Gatsby literally makes himself invaluable because he knows that the yacht will run aground on a sand bar, and Cody will be dependent on him. Gatsby makes a decision that changes the trajectory of his entire life.

C 2. It was indirectly due to Cody that Gatsby drank so little. Sometimes in the course of gay parties women used to rub champagne into his hair; for himself he formed the habit of letting liquor alone.
Gatsby's choice to avoid liquor shows that Gatsby likes to remain in control of situations. He also saw how alcohol was Cody's downfall, because it caused him to make poor decisions. Gatsby does not give in to inhibitions like the guests at his parties, but acts as a controlling architect of his own life.

A 3. "Who is this Gatsby anyhow?" demanded Tom suddenly. "Some big bootlegger?"
Tom begins his earnest inquiry into Gatsby's background at this moment. He pursues it aggressively, and eventually throws it all in Gatsby's face during the get-together at the Plaza Hotel, which leads to the accident and death of Myrtle.

D 4. "I wanted somebody who wouldn't gossip. Daisy comes over quite often — in the afternoons."
After months of having an open door to the community, Gatsby has made a decision to close his home to guests and even his servants, who could not be counted on for their discretion the way his criminal associates could be. Gatsby makes the decision to be singly focused on Daisy.

A 5. "'You two start on home, Daisy,' said Tom. 'In Mr. Gatsby's car.'
She looked at Tom, alarmed now, but he insisted with magnanimous scorn."
Tom's order to Daisy to return to Long Island with Gatsby and to use their drive to end their relationship spurs on the action, causing a chain reaction of events that leads to Myrtle's death.

D 6. "The God damned coward!" he whimpered. "He didn't even stop his car."
Believing he knows what happened at the scene of the accident, Tom makes a determination about Gatsby and his character. Tom is, of course, wrong, and does not fathom that Daisy is actually responsible for hitting and killing Myrtle.

The Great Gatsby Chapters 6-7

Reading Activity 5: Figurative Language

Anchor Standard	11th-12th Grade
CCRA.R.4	RL.11-12.4
CCRA.SL.1	SL.11-12.1

Objectives

Students will determine the meaning of words and phrases as they are used in the text, including figurative and connotative meanings.

Students will determine how figurative language contributes to meaning.

Directions

The following page has a passage from the text which includes examples of figurative language. This work-sheet can be done individually, as a whole-class activity, or in small groups. Discuss the answers as a whole class. Collect the worksheets and record the grades if you choose to do so.

Follow-Up/Assessment/Extension

Ask students to annotate instances of these types of figurative language as they read. Consider whether any particular type is associated with particular characters.

The Great Gatsby Chapters 6-7: Figurative Language

Answer the questions that correspond to the letters on the lines below. Explain how the figurative language helps create meaning.

"Come outside," he suggested to Gatsby, "I'd like you to have a look at the place."

I went with them out to the veranda. On the green Sound, stagnant in the heat, one small sail crawled slowly [A] toward the fresher sea. Gatsby's eyes followed it momentarily; he raised his hand and pointed across the bay.

"I'm right across from you."

"So you are."

Our eyes lifted over the rose-beds and the hot lawn and the weedy refuse of the dog-days along-shore [B]. Slowly the white wings of the boat [C] moved against the blue cool limit of the sky [D]. Ahead lay the scalloped ocean and the abounding blessed isles.

"There's sport for you," said Tom, nodding. "I'd like to be out there with him for about an hour."

A. The underlined section is what kind of figurative language?

____

Why is the mention of a sailboat significant?

B. Consider this visual imagery. What progression does it have?

____

How does the progression contribute to meaning in the passage? Does it seem positive or negative?

C. The underlined section is what kind of figurative language?

____

What does the image connote?

D. The underlined section is what kind of figurative language?

____

How does this particular action relate to larger themes in the novel?

E. How does the repetition of eyes and eye imagery relate to other points in the novel?

The Great Gatsby Chapters 6-7: Figurative Language Suggested Answers

"Come outside," he suggested to Gatsby, "I'd like you to have a look at the place."

I went with them out to the veranda. On the green Sound, stagnant in the heat, one small sail crawled slowly [A] toward the fresher sea. Gatsby's eyes followed it momentarily; he raised his hand and pointed across the bay.

"I'm right across from you."

"So you are."

Our eyes lifted over the rose-beds and the hot lawn and the weedy refuse of the dog-days along-shore [B]. Slowly the white wings of the boat [C] moved against the blue cool limit of the sky [D]. Ahead lay the scalloped ocean and the abounding blessed isles.

"There's sport for you," said Tom, nodding. "I'd like to be out there with him for about an hour."

A. The underlined section is what kind of figurative language?
The image of a sail "crawling" is personification.

Why is the mention of a sailboat significant?
Gatsby is associated with sailboats, particularly when he provides assistance to and meets Dan Cody.

B. Consider this visual imagery. What progression does it have?

The description moves from the manicured to the wild, from the beautiful ("rose-beds") to the ugly ("refuse").

How does the progression contribute to meaning in the passage? Does it seem positive or negative?
The progression is negative the further away from Tom's house one looks—literally, from beautiful gardens of roses to garbage. This suggests that the wealthy are the best people, and that beyond them, there is only trash.

C. The underlined section is what kind of figurative language?
The description of the boat's parts as white wings is a direct comparison or metaphor.

What does the image connote?
The imagery makes the boat sound like a bird, and birds are usually associated with freedom.

D. The underlined section is what kind of figurative language?
Again, this is a metaphor, since the comparison is direct.

How does this particular action relate to larger themes in the novel?
This passage could be read two ways—that the sky literally is the limit or that there are no limits (as in the idiom, the sky is the limit).

E. How does the repetition of eyes and eye imagery relate to other points in the novel?
Tom invites Gatsby outside to admire Tom's house, but the men look at the physical environment, literally the divide between the Eggs (and figuratively the divide between the classes) and they look at Gatsby's house. Much of the novel is about being looked at, either as a way to have value or because one is being judged (like the T.J. Eckleburg imagery).

The Great Gatsby Chapters 6-7

Reading Activity 6: Elements of Fiction & Literary Devices

Anchor Standard	11th-12th Grade
CCRA.R.1	RL.11-12.1
	RL.11-12.2
	RL.11-12.4
	RL.11-12.5
CCRA.SL.1	SL.11-12.1

Objective

Students will study and discuss passages from the text to examine symbol, motif and theme and explore how these create meaning in the text.

Directions

Use the following discussion questions as a guide to discussing symbol, motif and theme, in these chapters. You can give students the questions ahead of time and have them formulate answers prior to the class discussion or you can jump right in with a whole class discussion without student preparation if your students will handle that well.

As you hold the class discussion, be sure to include conversations defining symbol, motif and theme and explaining how these work together to advance meaning in the text.

Follow-Up/Assessment/Extension

After your discussion, ask students to look for recurrences of these symbols, motifs and themes in future chapters.

The Great Gatsby Chapters 6-7: Elements of Fiction & Literary Devices

1. One of the motifs in the novel is boats. Consider this passage:

It was a random shot, and yet the reporter's instinct was right. Gatsby's notoriety, spread about by the hundreds who had accepted his hospitality and so become authorities on his past, had increased all summer until he fell just short of being news. Contemporary legends such as the "underground pipe-line to Canada" attached themselves to him, and there was one persistent story that he didn't live in a house at all, but in a boat that looked like a house and was moved secretly up and down the Long Island shore. Just why these inventions were a source of satisfaction to James Gatz of North Dakota, isn't easy to say.

What is the connection between Gatsby and boats? Why is this rumor particularly apt?

2. One of the themes in the novel is becoming a self-made man. How does Gatsby accomplish this, and does it work successfully?

3. A motif in the novel is the weather. What is the weather like in Chapter 7? How does it contribute to meaning?

4. The concept of perception versus reality is a theme in the novel. In what ways does that appear in Chapter 6 and 7?

5. Why is Gatsby's response to Pammy significant? What does Pammy symbolize?

6. A major theme in the novel is how consumerism corrupts. Is Daisy corrupted? Why is it significant that she compares Gatsby to an advertisement?

The Great Gatsby Chapters 6-7:
Elements of Fiction & Literary Devices Suggested Answers

1. One of the motifs in the novel is boats. Consider this passage:

"It was a random shot, and yet the reporter's instinct was right. Gatsby's notoriety, spread about by the hundreds who had accepted his hospitality and so become authorities on his past, had increased all summer until he fell just short of being news. Contemporary legends such as the 'underground pipe-line to Canada' attached themselves to him, and there was one persistent story that he didn't live in a house at all, but in a boat that looked like a house and was moved secretly up and down the Long Island shore. Just why these inventions were a source of satisfaction to James Gatz of North Dakota, isn't easy to say."

What is the connection between Gatsby and boats? Why is this rumor particularly apt?
Gatsby changed his life and entire fortunes in a boat, warning Dan Cody about potential damage to his yacht. The yacht represented everything Gatz aspired to: "To the young Gatz, resting on his oars and looking up at the railed deck, the yacht represented all the beauty and glamour in the world."

2. One of the themes in the novel is becoming a self-made man. How does Gatsby accomplish this, and does it work successfully? Ultimately, what does Daisy think about it?
Gatsby accumulates his wealth through participating in organized crime, primarily bootlegging. Tom emphasizes this point in both Chapters 6 and 7 as a way to discredit Gatsby. Gatsby's wealth provides him with access to material things, but not to "class," in the social sense of the term. While people like Wolfsheim and Gatsby's party guests appreciate his wealth, ultimately Daisy does not. His participation in organized crime scares her and makes his "new money" lifestyle less legitimate than an "old money" lifestyle like Tom's.

3. A motif in the novel is the weather. What is the weather like in Chapter 7? How does it contribute to meaning?
The word "hot" is emphasized multiple times in the chapter, from the "hot whistles" to the train conductor's greetings: "Hot!" said the conductor to familiar faces. "Some weather! hot! hot! hot! Is it hot enough for you? Is it hot? Is it . . .?" In response to the heat, Daisy suggests going into the city. At the Plaza, they still find no relief from the oppressive heat, and it contributes to the confused, oppressive, volatile atmosphere.

4. The concept of perception versus reality is a theme in the novel. In what ways does that appear in Chapter 6 and 7?
In these chapters, multiple characters make wrong assumptions that lead to their demises. First is Myrtle, who mistakes Jordan for Daisy (realized that her eyes, wide with jealous terror, were fixed not on Tom, but on Jordan Baker, whom she took to be his wife) and erroneously believes that Tom has a different car. Gatsby believes that the past can be replicated and that Daisy has never loved anyone but him ("I'm going to fix everything just the way it was before," he said, nodding determinedly. "She'll see."). Tom erroneously believes that Gatsby—a romantic rival for his wife's affection—must be responsible for Myrtle's death.

5. Why is Gatsby's response to Pammy significant? What does Pammy symbolize?
Compared to Gatsby's reaction to Pammy, it is ironic how Daisy responds to her, calling her "You dream, you. You absolute little dream." Gatsby would likely wish to think of Pammy as a "dream," in that he might prefer that she didn't exist: "Gatsby and I in turn leaned down and took the small, reluctant hand. Afterward he kept looking at the child with surprise. I don't think he had ever really believed in its existence before." To Gatsby, Pammy is a symbol of the ways that Daisy is not his and how she is personally, romantically, sexually, and maritially linked to Tom.

6. A major theme in the novel is how consumerism corrupts. Why is it significant that Daisy compares Gatsby to an advertisement?
Daisy has already shown that she appreciates Gatsby's wealth, particularly in the scene when she visits his house and weeps at seeing his fine shirts. Daisy, whose voice is described as having money in it, is fully about conspicuous consumption. To compare Gatsby to an advertisement is apropos, as an advertisement is primarily a superficial promise to a customer. Gatsby only offers a superficial glimpse into his "brand"—who he is, how he conducts business and what business he conducts. Interestingly, the moment when she mentions the advertisement is when Tom becomes acutely aware of Daisy's infidelities, which suggests that she is corrupted.

The Great Gatsby Chapters 6-7

Reading Activity 7: Meaning and Inferences

Anchor Standard	11th-12th Grade
CCRA.R.1	RL.11-12.1
CCRA.SL.1	SL.11-12.1

Objective

Students will answer questions about selected passages from the text which require them to extract meaning or inferences from the text.

Directions

The following pages contain passages from Chapters 6-7 of *The Great Gatsby* and questions related to the passages that require close reading to answer. Students should answer the questions related to the passages.

This can be done as a whole-class activity, individually, or in small groups. If it is done individually or in small groups, come together as a class to discuss the answers to the questions.

Follow-Up/Assessment/Extension

Collect the worksheets for review and/or grading. Ask students to keep these as possible raw material for writing essays in the future.

The Great Gatsby Chapters 6-7: Meaning & Inferences 1

Read the passages and answer the related questions.

1. "He wanted nothing less of Daisy than that she should go to Tom and say: "I never loved you." After she had obliterated four years with that sentence they could decide upon the more practical measures to be taken. One of them was that, after she was free, they were to go back to Louisville and be married from her house—just as if it were five years ago."

What does returning to Louisville suggest about Gatsby's plans?

2. "I suppose he'd had the name ready for a long time, even then. His parents were shiftless and unsuccessful farm people—his imagination had never really accepted them as his parents at all. The truth was that Jay Gatsby of West Egg, Long Island, sprang from his Platonic conception of himself. He was a son of God – a phrase which, if it means anything, means just that – and he must be about His Father's business, the service of a vast, vulgar, and meretricious beauty. So he invented just the sort of Jay Gatsby that a seventeen-year-old boy would be likely to invent, and to this conception he was faithful to the end."

What, according to Nick, is the "truth" about Gatsby?

3. "He talked a lot about the past, and I gathered that he wanted to recover something, some idea of himself perhaps, that had gone into loving Daisy. His life had been confused and disordered since then, but if he could return to a certain starting place and go over it all slowly, he could find out what that thing was..."

What "thing" is that?

4. "Thirty – the promise of a decade of loneliness, a thinning list of single men to know, a thinning brief-case of enthusiasm, thinning hair. But there was Jordan beside me, who, unlike Daisy, was too wise ever to carry well-forgotten dreams from age to age. As we passed over the dark bridge her wan face fell lazily against my coat's shoulder and the formidable stroke of thirty died away with the reassuring pressure of her hand."

Why is Nick's recognition about his birthday apropos at this moment?

5. "She's not leaving me!" Tom's words suddenly leaned down over Gatsby. "Certainly not for a common swindler who'd have to steal the ring he put on her finger."

"I won't stand this!" cried Daisy. "Oh, please let's get out."

What does this suggest about Tom's view of marriage?

The Great Gatsby Chapters 6-7:
Meaning & Inferences 1 Suggested Answers

Read the passages and answer the related questions.

1. “He wanted nothing less of Daisy than that she should go to Tom and say: "I never loved you." After she had obliterated four years with that sentence they could decide upon the more practical measures to be taken. One of them was that, after she was free, they were to go back to Louisville and be married from her house—just as if it were five years ago.”

What does returning to Louisville suggest about Gatsby’s plans?
Gatsby is literally attempting to recover the past. He wants to take up where his dreams about Daisy left off, even though Daisy has been away from Louisville for five years. Gatsby’s goal is impossible, as he attempts to “fix everything the way it was before.” But, Daisy’s time with Tom, her feelings for him and her daughter cannot be so easily “obliterated” and made to no longer exist.

2. “I suppose he'd had the name ready for a long time, even then. His parents were shiftless and unsuccessful farm people—his imagination had never really accepted them as his parents at all. The truth was that Jay Gatsby of West Egg, Long Island, sprang from his Platonic conception of himself. He was a son of God – a phrase which, if it means anything, means just that – and he must be about His Father's business, the service of a vast, vulgar, and meretricious beauty. So he invented just the sort of Jay Gatsby that a seventeen-year-old boy would be likely to invent, and to this conception he was faithful to the end.”

What, according to Nick, is the “truth” about Gatsby?
The grammar of the sentence (and the repetition of “Jay Gatsby”) makes “truth” the antecedent to “this conception” to which “he was faithful to the end.” Gatsby’s made up persona is “truth” to him, it is the truer version of himself. He rejected his parentage because it felt inauthentic to who he was; to Gatsby, the “invention” actually is the “truth.”

3. “He talked a lot about the past, and I gathered that he wanted to recover something, some idea of himself perhaps, that had gone into loving Daisy. His life had been confused and disordered since then, but if he could return to a certain starting place and go over it all slowly, he could find out what that thing was…”
What “thing” is that?
The suggestion is that this missing “thing” would be not exactly class, but a kind of legitimacy that was part of Gatsby’s aspirations before he became involved in organized crime. Dan Cody was a mentor, reckless and wealthy, but a legitimate businessman. Meyer Wolfsheim as a mentor came after Gatsby met Daisy, and introduced “confus[ion]” and “disorder[…]” into Gatsby’s life. Daisy objects to this lack of legitimacy, and it means that Gatsby cannot fully possess her, unless he can go back to the beginning of their romance and do it over, but that is a doomed possibility.

4. "Thirty – the promise of a decade of loneliness, a thinning list of single men to know, a thinning brief-case of enthusiasm, thinning hair. But there was Jordan beside me, who, unlike Daisy, was too wise ever to carry well-forgotten dreams from age to age. As we passed over the dark bridge her wan face fell lazily against my coat's shoulder and the formidable stroke of thirty died away with the reassuring pressure of her hand."

Why is Nick's recognition about his birthday apropos at this moment?
Here Nick is resigning himself to a life of unhappiness that lacks fulfillment. He compares Jordan to Daisy—a realist to a romantic—and understands that romantic dreams are as impossible for him as they are for Gatsby.

5. " "She's not leaving me!" Tom's words suddenly leaned down over Gatsby. "Certainly not for a common swindler who'd have to steal the ring he put on her finger."

"I won't stand this!" cried Daisy. "Oh, please let's get out."

What does this suggest about Tom's view of marriage?
Like everything else in Tom's world, his view of marriage is commoditized, with a woman being an object—a prize—to possess. To Tom, Gatsby lacks the social status to be with Daisy. He "leaned down over Gatsby," as if he is socially superior. Tom is a businessman, and sees Gatsby as a "swindler," not legitimate, not completely legal. Tom sees the ultimate act of marriage in terms of currency and trade: to put a ring on her finger. Daisy is Tom's property.

The Great Gatsby Chapters 6-7: Meaning & Inferences 2

Read the passage and answer the related questions.

I hadn't gone twenty yards when I heard my name and Gatsby stepped from between two bushes into the path. I must have felt pretty weird by that time because I could think of nothing except the luminosity of his pink suit under the moon.

'What are you doing?' I inquired.

'Just standing here, old sport.'

Somehow that seemed a despicable occupation. For all I knew he was going to rob the house in a moment; I wouldn't have been surprised to see sinister faces, the faces of "Wolfsheim's people," behind him in the dark shrubbery.

"Did you see any trouble on the road?" he asked after a minute.

"Yes."

He hesitated.

"Was she killed?"

"Yes."

"I thought so; I told Daisy I thought so. It's better that the shock should all come at once. She stood it pretty well."

He spoke as if Daisy's reaction was the only thing that mattered.

1. What does the "luminosity" of Gatsby's suit connote?

2. What might "weird" suggest?

3. Why is it a "despicable occupation"?

4. How does Nick feel towards Gatsby here?

5. What does "as if" suggest about Nick's view of the night's events?

The Great Gatsby Chapters 6-7:
Meaning & Inferences 2 Suggested Answers

I hadn't gone twenty yards when I heard my name and Gatsby stepped from between two bushes into the path. I must have felt pretty weird by that time because I could think of nothing except the luminosity of his pink suit under the moon.

'What are you doing?' I inquired.

'Just standing here, old sport.'

Somehow that seemed a despicable occupation. For all I knew he was going to rob the house in a moment; I wouldn't have been surprised to see sinister faces, the faces of "Wolfsheim's people," behind him in the dark shrubbery.

"Did you see any trouble on the road?" he asked after a minute.

"Yes."

He hesitated.

"Was she killed?"

"Yes."

"I thought so; I told Daisy I thought so. It's better that the shock should all come at once. She stood it pretty well."

He spoke as if Daisy's reaction was the only thing that mattered.

1. What does the "luminosity" of Gatsby's suit connote?
Luminosity means the quality of brightness of an object. The glowing pink suit connects Gatsby to Daisy's windows which glow pink. Gatsby is watching in the darkness as Nick approaches, which connects to the scene early in the novel when Gatsby has his arms outstretched toward the green light on Daisy's dock. Like the green light, his suit has an illuminated quality. To Nick, the suit is highly noticeable, and it evokes Tom's comments about the suit as a way that designates Gatsby as unrefined and unsophisticated.

2. What might "weird" suggest?
Weird has two meanings, to feel uncharacteristically and to be influenced by supernatural causes. Here it suggests that the positive light in which Nick used to view Gatsby has been replaced with a more skeptical view. Nick does not feel like he normally does.

3. Why is it a "despicable occupation"?
To Nick, Gatsby's answer is not straightforward ("just standing here"), and he sees the nefarious side of Gatsby. The phrase also evokes Gatsby's real occupation, criminal.

4. How does Nick feel towards Gatsby here?
He sees Gatsby for what he is—a deluded, wealthy bootlegger—and the glamour and admiration he once saw is replaced by "sinister faces," which he fully expects.

5. What does "as if" suggest about Nick's view of the night's events?
The phrase indicates judgment, that Gatsby has the wrong view of the events. It shows how Nick's esteem for Gatsby falters because he realizes how singly focused on Daisy he is. He is concerned for Daisy, but disproportionately concerned about the woman she killed.

The Great Gatsby Chapters 6-7

Writing Activity 1: Moral Failure In The Great Gatsby

Anchor Standard	11th-12th Grade
CCRA.SL.1	SL.11-12.1, 1a-1d
CCRA.SL.3	SL. 11-12.4
CCRA.W.1	W. 11-12.2
CCRA.W.2	W. 11-12.4
CCRA.W.4	W. 11-12.5
CCRA.W.5	W. 11-12.7
	W. 11-12.9, 9b

Objectives

- Students will evaluate and analyze textual evidence to determine how the most dramatic chapters in the novel develop the theme of moral failure.

- Students will evaluate passages that show how characters engage in behavior that is not strictly moral.

- Students will examine language for biases and judgments.

- Students will write a composition in which they consider their analysis of relevant passages to answer the question, "How is moral failure significant in The Great Gatsby?"

Directions

The following series of worksheets and information organizers can be used by students individually, in small groups, or done partly as a whole-class activity. They are intended to guide students through the process of reading and thinking critically about information by ultimately answering the single question, "How is moral failure significant in The Great Gatsby?"

Preview the following pages. Determine the best way to have your particular class handle this assignment (individually, pairs, groups, whole-class, or some combination). A combination of group work (to do the analyzing of the text on the chart page) followed by individual work (to do the second and third pages of the assignment) would most likely be best to fulfill the standards listed for this assignment.

Follow-Up/Assessment/Extension

- The written assignment will be a good basis for assessment of the students' success with this assignment. Create a rubric explaining the criteria on which their written assignments will be evaluated.
- Ask students to consider other events in the novel that explore the gray area of morality. Ask students to think about the Valley of Ashes and the progression of Wilson's "sickness" as symptoms of moral failure.
- Have some students read/present their writing assignments to the class to practice more speaking/listening skills and to expose all students to each others' ideas.
- Use this assignment to discuss the idea of repercussions for behavior.

The Great Gatsby Chapters 6-7:
How Is Moral Failure Significant In The Great Gatsby?

As the omniscient eyes of T.J. Eckleburg loom over the bleak landscape of the Valley of Ashes, moral failure is a major theme in the novel. Though the narrator of the story claims to reserve judgment, the reader can detect that Nick understands that the characters surrounding him all participate in morally questionable acts.

Through close reading of the text, determine what the significance of moral failure in the novel is. Do all characters suffer the repercussions of their actions? Why or why not?

Using textual evidence from chapters 6-7, look for important but perhaps seemingly insignificant details to answer to the question: How is moral failure significant in The Great Gatsby?

To explore the significance of moral failure:

1. Identify passages and quotes which offer details or insights into how characters view their own morally questionable behaviors and if/when they suffer consequences of their behaviors.

2. Examine the context of your quotes.

3. Consider the connotation and denotation of key phrases in your quotes.

    a. Are there judgmental words or phrases?
    b. Does who a character interacts with matter?
    c. How does social class fit into excusing or punishing morally questionably behavior?
    d. Consider the perspective of the narrator. Is it biased?

4. Review passages for patterns to determine what the significance of moral failure is.

The Great Gatsby Chapters 6-7:
What Is The Significance Of Moral Failure In The Great Gatsby?

Use this chart (and additional pages, if needed) to collect, analyze and evaluate information about the trial.

Character	What moral transgressions has this character committed? Include textual evidence and page numbers.	Does the character (or other characters) justify their actions? How? Include textual evidence and page numbers.	Is there any consequence for the character's morally questionable behavior? Include textual evidence and page numbers.
Gatsby			
Nick			
Daisy			
Tom			

The Great Gatsby Chapters 6-7

Suggested Writing Assignments

Anchor Standard	11th-12th Grade
CCRA.W.1	W.11-12.1, 1a-1e
CCRA W.2	W.11-12.2, 2a-2f
CCRA.W.3	W.11-12.3, 3a-3e
CCRA.W.4	W.11-12.4
CCRA.W.5	W. 11-12.5

Objective

Students will be assigned or will choose one of a selection of writing assignments pertaining to Chapters 6-7 of *The Great Gatsby* to fulfill one or more of the standards listed above.

Directions

To provide you with maximum flexibility for differentiated instruction, the following page has a list of suggested writing assignments, all related to Chapters 6-7 of *The Great Gatsby*. Either assign individual students particular assignments to do or allow students to choose their own assignments.

A second page of "Quick Write" topics is also included.

Follow-Up/Assessment/Extension

- Have dramatic readings of students' narratives or poems.
- Create a "reading room" space in your classroom where students can donate their writing assignments for others in the class to read.
- Allow students to do more than one assignment if they want to.
- Use the "left-over" assignments (not chosen for this activity) as topics for journal entries.

The Great Gatsby Chapters 6-7: Creative Analytical Writing Assignments

1. Write a letter from Gatsby at college home to his parents. Incorporate details from the text.

2. Write a eulogy by Gatsby for Dan Cody.

3. Write a scene between Gatsby and Nick in which Gatsby explains why he does not drink alcohol.

4. Write a description of the past that Gatsby wants to repeat.

5. Write a letter from Daisy to Pammy about how to choose a husband.

6. Describe the life out west that Myrtle dreamed about when she was more happily married.

7. Write a newspaper account of Myrtle's accident.

8. Write an account of what happened that caused Tom and Daisy to leave Chicago.

9. During the confrontation between Gatsby and Tom at the hotel, write a paragraph that describes what Jordan is thinking.

10. Write the dialogue between Tom and Daisy as they are in their kitchen during the night of the accident.

The Great Gatsby Chapters 6-7: Quick-Write Writing Assignments

1. Why doesn't Daisy like Gatsby's party?
2. Why did Gatsby drop out of college?
3. Does Gatsby really love Daisy?
4. Who treats Daisy more like a possession, Gatsby or Tom?
5. What is Nick unable to vocalize at the end of Chapter 6?
6. What do Wilson and Tom have in common?
7. How does the green light symbolize the American Dream?
8. Why does Gatsby defend his business against Tom's criticisms?
9. Which is a more important mentor for Gatsby: Dan Cody or Meyer Wolfsheim?
10. When Nick sees Tom and Daisy in their kitchen talking, what does he recognize that this means for Gatsby's dream?

NOTES
THE GREAT GATSBY

MATERIALS: CHAPTERS 8-9

THE GREAT GATSBY

Reading Activity 1: True or False

Reading Activity 2: Analyzing Passages

Reading Activity 3: Direct And Indirect Characterization

Reading Activity 4: Action, Character, Decision

Reading Activity 5: Figurative Language

Reading Activity 6: Elements of Fiction & Literary Devices

Reading Activity 7: Meaning and Inferences

Writing Activity 1: Is Nick A Reliable Narrator?

Suggested Writing Assignments

Quick-Write Assignments

The Great Gatsby Chapters 8-9
Reading Activity 1: True or False?

Anchor Standard	11th-12th Grade
CCRA.R.1	RL.11-12.1
CCRA.SL1	SL.11-12.1
CCRA SL.4	SL.11-12.4

Objectives

- Students will be able to cite the parts of the text that support their analysis of what the text says or infers.
- Students will consider statements about the text, determine whether those statements are true or false, and will give textual evidence supporting their choices.
- Students will work together in small groups to discuss, analyze, and evaluate the statements made.
- Students will evaluate the analytical work of their peers.

Directions

Prior to reading Chapters 8-9: Give students (or post) the following list of statements about the chapters, and explain to students that they should read Chapters 8-9 to find out if these statements are true or false:

Gatsby wanted to be at Oxford.
After the war, Gatsby returned to Louisville.
Nick actually disapproved of Gatsby.
Nick says he was just an acquaintance of Gatsby.
Tom believes that Gatsby got what he deserved.
Owl-eyes is an unexpected attendee at Gatsby's burial.

After reading Chapters 8-9: The worksheets on the following pages can be done by students individually, in small groups, or as a whole class. Below are directions to use the questions as a group activity to fulfill more state standards:

- Cut the worksheet apart, making each question and answer box a slip.
- Divide your class into six groups and give one question and a True/False evaluation form to each group. Tell students they are to discuss the statement and determine if the statement is true or false, supporting their decision with evidence from the text. Tell them their answers will be evaluated on the criteria given on the evaluation form.
- Give students ample time to discuss the statements and record their answers.
- Have the groups swap True or False question slips so that each group can evaluate another group's answer. The group should fill in the number of the question they are evaluating, decide how well the answer fulfills the criteria listed, and fill out the form accordingly.
- Repeat the previous step until all the groups have evaluated each others' answers.
- Collect the evaluations and answer slips.

The Great Gatsby Chapters 8-9: True or False?

Write *True* or *False* in the blank next to each statement. Below the statement, explain why you chose true or false, referencing the text to support your choices.

__________ 1. Gatsby wanted to be at Oxford.

__________ 2. After the war, Gatsby returned to Louisville.

__________ 3. Nick actually disapproved of Gatsby.

_________ 4. Nick says he was just an acquaintance of Gatsby.

_________ 5. Tom believes that Gatsby got what he deserved.

__________ 6.Owl-eyes is an unexpected attendee at Gatsby's burial.

The Great Gatsby Chapters 8-9 True or False? Evaluation

List Your Group's Members: Your Group's Question # _______

__________________ __________________ __________________

__________________ __________________ __________________

1 = No, Not At All **2** = A Little **3** = Some **4** = Yes **5** = Yes, Very Well

Evaluation of Question # ___
Does the explanation support the answer of true or false? 1 2 3 4 5
Is there good textual evidence to support the answer? 1 2 3 4 5
Is the answer clearly stated? 1 2 3 4 5
Total Score ________ of a possible 15 points

Evaluation of Question # ___
Does the explanation support the answer of true or false? 1 2 3 4 5
Is there good textual evidence to support the answer? 1 2 3 4 5
Is the answer clearly stated? 1 2 3 4 5
Total Score ________ of a possible 15 points

Evaluation of Question # ___
Does the explanation support the answer of true or false? 1 2 3 4 5
Is there good textual evidence to support the answer? 1 2 3 4 5
Is the answer clearly stated? 1 2 3 4 5
Total Score ________ of a possible 15 points

Evaluation of Question # ___
Does the explanation support the answer of true or false? 1 2 3 4 5
Is there good textual evidence to support the answer? 1 2 3 4 5
Is the answer clearly stated? 1 2 3 4 5
Total Score ________ of a possible 15 points

Evaluation of Question # ___
Does the explanation support the answer of true or false? 1 2 3 4 5
Is there good textual evidence to support the answer? 1 2 3 4 5
Is the answer clearly stated? 1 2 3 4 5
Total Score ________ of a possible 15 points

The Great Gatsby Chapters 8-9: True or False? Suggested Answers

Write *True* or *False* in the blank next to each statement. Below the statement, explain why you chose true or false, referencing the text to support your choices.

FALSE 1. Gatsby wanted to be at Oxford.

Though it is part of his semi-autobiographical personal narrative, "after the Armistice he tried frantically to get home, but some complication or misunderstanding sent him to Oxford instead." Gatsby knows that Daisy feels an urgent need to be with him; ultimately she writes to him at Oxford and then moves on to a relationship with Tom.

TRUE 2. After the war, Gatsby returned to Louisville.

Gatsby misses Daisy and arrives when she is out of town, making "a miserable but irresistible journey to Louisville on the last of his army pay." After staying a week, he leaves and has a bad feeling: "He left feeling that if he had searched harder, he might have found her — that he was leaving her behind."

TRUE 3. Nick actually disapproved of Gatsby.

Nick pays Gatsby a compliment, saying that he is worth the whole bunch of them (Daisy, Tom, etc.), and follows quickly with narration stating that he "disapproved of him from beginning to end."

FALSE 4. Nick says he was just an acquaintance of Gatsby.

In response to Mr. Gatz's question about how Nick knew Gatsby, Nick responds "We were close friends." This may not be true, or it becomes more true as Nick feels empathy toward Gatsby after his death, or he says it to placate Mr. Gatz.

TRUE 5. Tom believes that Gatsby got what he deserved.

As Nick confirms his suspicion that Tom told Wilson that Gatsby owned the yellow car, Tom justifies his actions: "That fellow had it coming to him. He threw dust into your eyes just like he did in Daisy's, but he was a tough one." He shows no remorse for Gatsby's death, and stands on the principle of the "truth," which he is misinformed about.

TRUE 6. Owl-eyes is an unexpected attendee at Gatsby's burial.

The odd yet perceptive party guest shows up for the burial and remarks on how the party guests showed up in great numbers for parties, but not for a funeral. He offers bittersweet condolences: ""The poor son-of-a-bitch."

The Great Gatsby Chapters 8-9

Reading Activity 2: Analyzing Passages

Anchor Standard	11th-12th Grade
CCRA.R.6	RL.11-12.1
	RL.11-12.4
CCRA.SL.1	SL.11-12.1

Objectives

- Students will cite strong and thorough textual evidence to support analysis of what the text says explicitly as well as inferences drawn from the text, including determining where the text leaves matters uncertain.
- Determine the meaning of words and phrases as they are used in the text, including figurative and connotative meanings; analyze the impact of specific word choices on meaning and tone, including words with multiple meanings or language that is particularly fresh, engaging, or beautiful.
- Analyze a case in which grasping a point of view requires distinguishing what is directly stated in a text from what is really meant (e.g., satire, sarcasm, irony, or understatement).
- Students will analyze the impact of specific word choices on meaning and tone.

Directions

On the pages that follow, there are 8 passages to analyze, each with a question or questions to guide the process. There are many ways to use these questions:

- You could use them as a worksheet for all students to complete individually.
- You could use the worksheet as your guide in a whole-class discussion. Have students turn to the first passage in the book, read it, and then ask the question(s) orally. Repeat through all 8 questions.
- You could assign one passage to each of 8 different groups of students, for the students to discuss and come up with responses to the question(s). Then hold a whole-class discussion.
- You could read the passage and then see which student can find the passage first (to practice skimming skills). Then follow up with the questions(s) and discussion.
- You could have students choose one or two questions to respond to in writing in their notebooks or journals.

Follow-Up/Assessment/Extension

- Ask students to gather passages that relate to passages included here because they share the same motif, word use or images.
- Have students write about the two passages where Nick imagines the already deceased Gatsby speaking to him.
- Have students pick out other passages in this chapters that show interesting word usage, descriptions, or lack of clarity.
- As an introduction to this activity and these chapters, ask students to write about showing respect for other people. Who shows respect in these chapters? Who avoids respect and responsibility?

The Great Gatsby Chapters 8-9 Analyzing Passages

Answer the questions following the quotations completely.

1. "I couldn't sleep all night; a fog-horn was groaning incessantly on the Sound, and I tossed half-sick between grotesque reality and savage, frightening dreams. Toward dawn I heard a taxi go up Gatsby's drive, and immediately I jumped out of bed and began to dress — I felt that I had something to tell him, something to warn him about, and morning would be too late."

   How does this suggest foreshadowing?

2. "It was this night that he told me the strange story of his youth with Dan Cody — told it to me because 'Jay Gatsby' had broken up like glass against Tom's hard malice, and the long secret extravaganza was played out. I think that he would have acknowledged anything now, without reserve, but he wanted to talk about Daisy."

   Why is "acknowledged" significant here?

3. "It excited him, too, that many men had already loved Daisy — it increased her value in his eyes. He felt their presence all about the house, pervading the air with the shades and echoes of still vibrant emotions."

   What does this suggest about how Gatsby views Daisy?

4. "I can't describe to you how surprised I was to find out I loved her, old sport. I even hoped for a while that she'd throw me over, but she didn't, because she was in love with me too. She thought I knew a lot because I knew different things from her. . . . Well, there I was, 'way off my ambitions, getting deeper in love every minute, and all of a sudden I didn't care. What was the use of doing great things if I could have a better time telling her what I was going to do?"

   What does this show about how Gatsby relates to time?

5. "I wanted to get somebody for him. I wanted to go into the room where he lay and reassure him: 'I'll get somebody for you, Gatsby. Don't worry. Just trust me and I'll get somebody for you ——'"

   Why does Nick want to "get somebody" for Gatsby? What does that mean?

6. "Next morning I sent the butler to New York with a letter to Wolfsheim, which asked for information and urged him to come out on the next train. That request seemed superfluous when I wrote it. I was sure he'd start when he saw the newspapers, just as I was sure there'd be a wire from Daisy before noon — but neither a wire nor Mr. Wolfsheim arrived; no one arrived except more police and photographers and newspaper men. When the butler brought back Wolfsheim's answer I began to have a feeling of defiance, of scornful solidarity between Gatsby and me against them all."

   What does Nick feel "defian[t]" about?

7. "After that I felt a certain shame for Gatsby — one gentleman to whom I telephoned implied that he had got what he deserved. However, that was my fault, for he was one of those who used to sneer most bitterly at Gatsby on the courage of Gatsby's liquor, and I should have known better than to call him."

   What specifically does Nick feel shame about?

8. "You said a bad driver was only safe until she met another bad driver? Well, I met another bad driver, didn't I? I mean it was careless of me to make such a wrong guess. I thought you were rather an honest, straightforward person. I thought it was your secret pride."

   What is Jordan intimating about Nick?

The Great Gatsby Chapters 8-9 Analyzing Passages Suggested Answers

Answer the questions following the quotations completely.

1. "I couldn't sleep all night; a fog-horn was groaning incessantly on the Sound, and I tossed half-sick between grotesque reality and savage, frightening dreams. Toward dawn I heard a taxi go up Gatsby's drive, and immediately I jumped out of bed and began to dress — I felt that I had something to tell him, something to warn him about, and morning would be too late." How does this suggest foreshadowing?
   The connection with the maritme/boat motif connects the passage directly to Gatsby. The point of a fog-horn is to warn boats of unseen dangers. Here the "groaning" that is "incessant" and "grotesque" signals the unseen threat to Gatsby of Wilson's vendetta. The allusion to "savage, frightening dreams" also suggests that Gatsby should abandon his dream, which he is reluctant to do.

2. "It was this night that he told me the strange story of his youth with Dan Cody — told it to me because "Jay Gatsby" had broken up like glass against Tom's hard malice, and the long secret extravaganza was played out. I think that he would have acknowledged anything now, without reserve, but he wanted to talk about Daisy."
   Why is "acknowledged" significant here?
   Throughout the novel, there are moments of the authentic Gatsby and the "Great Gatsby," or this larger than life invented persona that—to Gatsby—is "true." "Acknowledged" suggests that Gatsby is aware of the difference between his public face and private, truer identity.

3. "It excited him, too, that many men had already loved Daisy — it increased her value in his eyes. He felt their presence all about the house, pervading the air with the shades and echoes of still vibrant emotions." What does this suggest about how Gatsby views Daisy?
   Literally the passage addresses how Gatsby sees Daisy ("in his eyes"), so she exists as a function of that and not as a separate unique individual with intrinsic "value." Her "value" is relative to how he perceives her, and like any commodity in a capitalist system, more competition for a good raises its value in the marketplace.

4. "I can't describe to you how surprised I was to find out I loved her, Old Sport. I even hoped for a while that she'd throw me over, but she didn't, because she was in love with me too. She thought I knew a lot because I knew different things from her. . . . Well, there I was, 'way off my ambitions, getting deeper in love every minute, and all of a sudden I didn't care. What was the use of doing great things if I could have a better time telling her what I was going to do?" What does this show about how Gatsby relates to time?
   Gatsby shows that his is future-oriented, as if he projects into the future and creates a reality that he believes in. The comparison of "doing great things" to "telling her what I was going to do" highlights this future orientation. Gatsby is uncomfortable with his present circumstances—not having wealth or status.

5. "I wanted to get somebody for him. I wanted to go into the room where he lay and reassure him: 'I'll get somebody for you, Gatsby. Don't worry. Just trust me and I'll get somebody for you ——'" Why does Nick want to "get somebody" for Gatsby? What does that mean?
   Nick is committed to finding someone who knew Gatsby personally and feels a calling to mourn for him. Most people know Gatsby in an impersonal way, merely as a somewhat infamous, mythologized public figure. To Nick, finding someone who cared about Gatsby in this way would make him less "great" and more legitimate and human.

6. "Next morning I sent the butler to New York with a letter to Wolfsheim, which asked for information and urged him to come out on the next train. That request seemed superfluous when I wrote it. I was sure he'd start when he saw the newspapers, just as I was sure there'd be a wire from Daisy before noon — but neither a wire nor Mr. Wolfsheim arrived; no one arrived except more police and photographers and newspaper men. When the butler brought back Wolfsheim's answer I began to have a feeling of defiance, of scornful solidarity between Gatsby and me against them all." What does Nick feel "defian[t]" about?
   What is striking in this passage is that Nick creates a dichotomy of "us" versus "them," and he includes Wolfsheim and Daisy in the same category. Here Nick is "defian[t]" against the propriety and politeness that social custom dictates that he show, but he is "scornful" or openly showing contempt. He goes against his own moral code—not to judge others.

7. "After that I felt a certain shame for Gatsby — one gentleman to whom I telephoned implied that he had got what he deserved. However, that was my fault, for he was one of those who used to sneer most bitterly at Gatsby on the courage of Gatsby's liquor, and I should have known better than to call him." What specifically does Nick feel shame about?
   Shame is a painful emotion caused by a strong sense of guilt, embarrassment, unworthiness, or disgrace. For same to exist, there has to be some "other" frame (like laws, rules for behavior, religion) for one to understand and filter his or her own experience through. Here this random party guest serves as the moral compass—an external frame—for reckoning Gatsby's life. It shows how little regard his guests had for him.

8. "You said a bad driver was only safe until she met another bad driver? Well, I met another bad driver, didn't I? I mean it was careless of me to make such a wrong guess. I thought you were rather an honest, straightforward person. I thought it was your secret pride." What is Jordan intimating about Nick?
   Jordan intimates that Nick is a "bad driver." She is suggesting that he is neither "honest" nor "straightforward." This is likely true, as Nick is never associated with driving, but is depicted as a passenger. The reader is left to take Nick's word for his character or lack thereof it.

The Great Gatsby Chapters 8-9

Reading Activity 3: Direct and Indirect Characterization

Anchor Standard	11th-12th Grade
CCRA.R.1	RL.11-12.1
CCRA.SL.1	SL.11-12.1

Objective

Using textual evidence, students will explore the subtleties of character development.

Directions

The direct vs. indirect characterization worksheet on the following page could be used in many ways, completed by small groups of students, individual students, or as a whole class activity.

Students can use their current observations about the characters to understand ways that important information about characters is conveyed directly or indirectly.

Students may (and should) use their books to skim through the chapter to refresh their memories or gather more information about the characters.

After students complete the worksheets discuss students' answers as a whole class. Collect the worksheets for grading, if you choose, or have students put them in their notebooks for further study.

Follow-Up/Assessment/Extension

Revisit this assignment later in the unit and discuss how characters, especially Daisy, "prove" the indirect characterization that readers inferred.

The Great Gatsby Chapters 8-9
Reading Activity 3: Direct vs. Indirect Characterization

Characterization, or the development of characters in a work of fiction, can be direct or indirect. Direct characterization is revealing aspects of character directly to the reader via a narrator, the character him or herself or from another character. Indirect characterization requires readers to infer what a character is like through the character's thoughts, action, diction, appearance and interactions with others.

Complete the chart, using actual quotes when asked and noting page numbers.

Character	Direct Characterization Quote	Indirect Characterization Quote	Indirect Characterization Inference
Nick			
Gatsby			
Tom			
Wilson			
Jordan			
Wolfsheim			
Owl-eyes			

The Great Gatsby Chapters 8-9
Reading Activity 3: Direct vs. Indirect Characterization

Characterization, or the development of characters in a work of fiction, can be direct or indirect. Direct characterization is revealing aspects of character directly to the reader via a narrator, the character him or herself or from another character. Indirect characterization requires readers to infer what a character is like through the character's thoughts, action, diction, appearance and interactions with others.

Answers will vary. There are so many different possibilities, it's impossible to make a definitive answer key. Evaluate each of your own students' responses individually.

Character	Direct Characterization Quote	Indirect Characterization Quote	Indirect Characterization Inference
Nick			
Gatsby			
Tom			
Wilson			
Jordan			
Wolfsheim			
Owl-eyes			

The Great Gatsby Chapters 8-9

Reading Activity 4: Action, Character, Decision

Anchor Standard	11th-12th Grade
CCRA.R.1	RL.11-12.1
CCRA.SL.1	SL.11-12.1

Objective

Students will identify particular lines of dialogue or incidents in the story that propel the action, reveal aspects of character, or provoke a decision.

Directions

The following page contains passages from Chapters 8-9 of *The Great Gatsby*. Students should determine whether the passages advance the action, reveal aspects of a character, or provoke a decision.

This can be done as a whole-class activity, individually, or in small groups.

Follow-Up/Assessment/Extension

Have students skim Chapters 8-9 in the text to find one example of a passage that propels the action, one that reveals aspects of a character, and one that provokes a decision. Again, this could be done individually or as a group. This activity can be a quick prompt for starting class discussion of a reading assignment.

The Great Gatsby Chapters 8-9: Action, Character, Decision

Write **A** (for Action) **C** (for Character) or **D** (for Decision) in the blank next to each to identify whether the passage/statement advances the action, tells us more about a character, or provokes a decision. On the lines under each question, provide a short explanation of your choice.

____ 1. "As a matter of fact, he had no such facilities — he had no comfortable family standing behind him, and he was liable at the whim of an impersonal government to be blown anywhere about the world."

____ 2. "He had intended, probably, to take what he could and go — but now he found that he had committed himself to the following of a grail."

____ 3. "And all the time something within her was crying for a decision. She wanted her life shaped now, immediately — and the decision must be made by some force — of love, of money, of unquestionable practicality — that was close at hand."

____ 4. "When the butler brought back Wolfsheim's answer I began to have a feeling of defiance, of scornful solidarity between Gatsby and me against them all."

____ 5. "'I don't think she ever loved him.' Gatsby turned around from a window and looked at me challengingly."

____ 6. "'I can't do it — I can't get mixed up in it,' he said."

The Great Gatsby Chapters 8-9:
Action, Character, Decision Suggested Answers

Write **A** (for Action) **C** (for Character) or **D** (for Decision) in the blank next to each to identify whether the passage/statement advances the action, tells us more about a character, or provokes a decision. On the lines under each question, provide a short explanation of your choice.

C 1. "As a matter of fact, he had no such facilities — he had no comfortable family standing behind him, and he was liable at the whim of an impersonal government to be blown anywhere about the world."
Gatsby, being in the military, is not free to be with Daisy when he pleases. His inability to return from France before attending Oxford led to Daisy giving up on him and consequently marrying Tom.

A 2. "He had intended, probably, to take what he could and go — but now he found that he had committed himself to the following of a grail."
Even to his own surprise, Gatsby falls in love with Daisy, or at least the idea of her. He recognizes his life is "committed" to pursuit of "a grail," or Daisy. All the choices that Gatsby makes—from earning wealth through organized crime to where to live is informed by this ambition.

D 3. "And all the time something within her was crying for a decision. She wanted her life shaped now, immediately — and the decision must be made by some force — of love, of money, of unquestionable practicality — that was close at hand."
In the absence of clear expectations about a relationship and marriage with Gatsby, Daisy felt the pressures of the social scene and recognized that she wanted to move her life forward, ultimately marrying Tom.

D 4. "When the butler brought back Wolfsheim's answer I began to have a feeling of defiance, of scornful solidarity between Gatsby and me against them all."
Nick changes his assumptions about the people who have disappointed him; he makes a decision to have loyalty to Gatsby, even if that means turning his back on his class and social loyalties.

C 5. "'I don't think she ever loved him.' Gatsby turned around from a window and looked at me challengingly."
Gatsby, despite seeing Daisy protest his claims that she has only loved him, and despite meeting Pammy, shows how willfully deluded he is in believing in his dream and idealized view of Daisy at all costs.

A 6. "'I can't do it — I can't get mixed up in it,' he said."
Despite claiming to have "made" Gatsby, Wolfsheim declines attending his funeral. He attempts to make a distinction between his personal feelings and his business obligations. His refusal to attend leads to a sad, sparsely attended funeral.

The Great Gatsby Chapters 8-9

Reading Activity 5: Figurative Language

Anchor Standard	11th-12th Grade
CCRA.R.4	RL.11-12.4
CCRA.SL.1	SL.11-12.1

Objectives

- Students will determine the meaning of words and phrases as they are used in the text, including figurative and connotative meanings.
- Students will determine how figurative language contributes to meaning.

Directions

The following page has a passage from the text which includes examples of figurative language. This worksheet can be done individually, as a whole-class activity, or in small groups. Discuss the answers as a whole class. Collect the worksheets and record the grades if you choose to do so.

Follow-Up/Assessment/Extension

Ask students to annotate instances of these types of figurative language as they read. Consider whether any particular type is associated with particular characters.

The Great Gatsby Chapters 8-9: Figurative Language

Irony is the contrast between what is expected or what appears to be and what actually is. Irony can be verbal (a contrast using language) or situational (a contrast using an unexpected result). Explain how irony helps create meaning in the passages below

1. His gorgeous pink rag of a suit made a bright spot of color against the white steps, and I thought of the night when I first came to his ancestral home, three months before.

2. The minister glanced several times at his watch, so I took him aside and asked him to wait for half an hour. But it wasn't any use. Nobody came.

3. "If he'd of lived, he'd of been a great man. A man like James J. Hill. He'd of helped build up the country."
"That's true," I said, uncomfortably.

4. "I couldn't get to the house," he remarked.
"Neither could anybody else."
"Go on!" He started. "Why, my God! they used to go there by the hundreds." He took off his glasses and wiped them again, outside and in.

5. "What I called up about was a pair of shoes I left there. I wonder if it'd be too much trouble to have the butler send them on. You see, they're tennis shoes, and I'm sort of helpless without them. My address is care of B. F. ——"

The Great Gatsby Chapters 8-9: Figurative Language Suggested Answers

Irony is the contrast between what is expected or what appears to be and what actually is. Irony can be verbal (a contrast using language) or situational (a contrast using an unexpected result). Explain how irony helps create meaning in the passages below.

1. His gorgeous pink rag of a suit made a bright spot of color against the white steps, and I thought of the night when I first came to his ancestral home, three months before.
The ironic part of the passage is the description of Gatsby's home as "ancestral." Gatsby and his "new money" gained from organized crime are as far away from "ancestral" as is probably possible. Perhaps the homes in East Egg could be considered "ancestral" as they are part of moneyed families for generations, but Gatsby has no ties to the home or the land. The mention of his garish "pink rag of a suit" reminds the reader that Gatsby has wealth but not the class of a gentrified family.

2. The minister glanced several times at his watch, so I took him aside and asked him to wait for half an hour. But it wasn't any use. Nobody came.
This is an example of situational irony—Gatsby had welcomed many, many guests into his home for parties, but none show for his funeral.

3. "If he'd of lived, he'd of been a great man. A man like James J. Hill. He'd of helped build up the country."
"That's true," I said, uncomfortably.
The irony in this passage is Mr. Gatz's comparison of Gatsby to James J. Hill, a leading businessman in the railroad industry and philanthropist. Gatsby, of course, did not have a legitimate business building America's infrastructure, but an illegal business supplying alcohol during Prohibition. Nick agrees out of politeness; being a Midwesterner, he would know who James J. Hill was.

4. "I couldn't get to the house," he remarked.
"Neither could anybody else."
"Go on!" He started. "Why, my God! they used to go there by the hundreds." He took off his glasses and wiped them again, outside and in.
Here Nick's comment is ironic, bordering on sarcastic. Conceivably Owl-eyes has a legitimate excuse for missing the first part of the funeral. Nick's reply is ironic in that it is not the expected response, which would be that no one showed up. The response highlights the total lack of care that people who took advantage of Gatsby's hospitality showed upon his death.

5. "What I called up about was a pair of shoes I left there. I wonder if it'd be too much trouble to have the butler send them on. You see, they're tennis shoes, and I'm sort of helpless without them. My address is care of B. F. ——"
Situational irony abounds here as Klipspringer behaves as if forgotten tennis shoes are a more important and urgent matter than Gatsby's murder. The use of the word "helpless" further illuminates Klipspringer's total selfishness and total lack of caring toward Gatsby.

The Great Gatsby Chapters 8-9

Reading Activity 6: Elements of Fiction & Literary Devices

Anchor Standard	11th-12th Grade
CCRA.R.1	RL.11-12.1
	RL.11-12.2
	RL.11-12.4
	RL.11-12.5
CCRA.SL.1	SL.11-12.1

Objective

Students will study and discuss passages from the text to examine symbol, motif and theme and explore how these create meaning in the text.

Directions

Use the following discussion questions as a guide to discussing symbol, motif and theme, in these chapters. You can give students the questions ahead of time and have them formulate answers prior to the class discussion or you can jump right in with a whole class discussion without student preparation if your students will handle that well.

As you hold the class discussion, be sure to include conversations defining symbol, motif and theme and explaining how these work together to advance meaning in the text.

Follow-Up/Assessment/Extension

After your discussion, ask students to look for recurrences of these symbols, motifs and themes in future chapters.

The Great Gatsby Chapters 8-9: Elements of Fiction & Literary Devices

1. One of the motifs in the novel is the weather. At what point in the season does this chapter take place? With what details does Fitzgerald convey that?

2. Chapters 8 and 9 have the most interruptions by Nick that draw attention to his role as narrator. Explain the significance of this shift in perspective: "Now I want to go back a little and tell what happened at the garage after we left there the night before"

3. Consider the motif of seeing and eyes in the novel. Assess this quote:

"Standing behind him, Michaelis saw with a shock that he was looking at the eyes of Doctor T. J. Eckleburg, which had just emerged, pale and enormous, from the dissolving night.
'God sees everything,' repeated Wilson.
'That's an advertisement,' Michaelis assured him."

Does Wilson's understanding of Doctor T. J. Eckleburg align with the general idea of the motif or diverge from it?

4. Compare this scene to the scene where Nick attempts (and succeeds) to gain access to Meyer Wolfsheim. What does the difference between these encounters suggest about the very wealthy?

"I called up Daisy half an hour after we found him, called her instinctively and without hesitation. But she and Tom had gone away early that afternoon, and taken baggage with them.
'Left no address?'
'No.'
'Say when they'd be back?'
'No.'
'Any idea where they are? How I could reach them?'
'I don't know. Can't say.'"

5. How does Mr, Gatz reflect the American Dream?

6. What is the source of the conflict between Nick and Jordan?

The Great Gatsby Chapters 8-9:
Elements of Fiction & Literary Devices Suggested Answers

1. One of the motifs in the novel is the weather. At what point in the season does this chapter take place? With what details does Fitzgerald convey that?
Fitzgerald directly addresses a change in the weather: "The night had made a sharp difference in the weather and there was an autumn flavor in the air." In the wake of the tragedies, summer gives way to fall. This connects Gatsby to the last time he "lost" Daisy, which was also in the fall: "On the last afternoon before he went abroad, he sat with Daisy in his arms for a long, silent time. It was a cold fall day, with fire in the room and her cheeks flushed."

2. Chapters 8 and 9 have the most interruptions by Nick that draw attention to his role as narrator. Explain the significance of this shift in perspective: "Now I want to go back a little and tell what happened at the garage after we left there the night before."
This shift positions Nick as an unreliable narrator. He was not present, but relates knowledge of incidents anyway. It calls into question the perspective in the entire narrative.

3. Consider the motif of seeing and eyes in the novel. Assess this quote:
"Standing behind him, Michaelis saw with a shock that he was looking at the eyes of Doctor T. J. Eckleburg, which had just emerged, pale and enormous, from the dissolving night.

'God sees everything,' repeated Wilson.

'That's an advertisement,' Michaelis assured him."

Does Wilson's understanding of Doctor T. J. Eckleburg align with the general idea of the motif or diverge from it?
Wilson's view of Doctor T. J. Eckleburg as God does diverge from the primary way that the motif is presented—yes, as seeing and in some ways omniscient, but more like a social conscience than a particularly religious one. The larger concept of religious dogma is absent from the text.

4. Compare this scene to the scene where Nick attempts (and succeeds) to gain access to Meyer Wolfsheim. What does the difference between these encounters suggest about the very wealthy?

"I called up Daisy half an hour after we found him, called her instinctively and without hesitation. But she and Tom had gone away early that afternoon, and taken baggage with them.
'Left no address?'
'No.'
'Say when they'd be back?'
'No.'
'Any idea where they are? How I could reach them?'
'I don't know. Can't say.'"

With insistence, Nick eventually gets past the secretary who is attempting to be a gatekeeper by insisting that Wolfsheim is in Chicago. Nick fails to be in touch with Daisy, who along with Tom, has a pattern of fleeing from problems for which they are culpable. This difference suggests that the rich, upper class can abscond and make others clean up their messes.

5. How does Mr, Gatz reflect the American Dream?
As a member of the lower class (similar to Myrtle), he is unsophisticated enough to believe in the American Dream, or the idea that a man can become self-made and wealthy and therefore "successful." He is conflicted when he encounters Gatsby's home and the reality of his death: "his grief began to be mixed with an awed pride." This "pride" is for the belief that his son achieved this impossible dream.

6. What is the source of the conflict between Nick and Jordan?
Nick admits that he s "half in love" with Jordan near the end of the novel. However, the internal conflict in Nick that pits the East versus the West and morality versus immorality is externalized in his failed romance with Jordan. Ultimately he must reject the East to keep his own values system intact, and that includes rejecting Jordan and her morally ambiguous lifestyle. He is too keenly observant to be one of the lesser males she surrounds herself with to maintain a semblance of control and to allow her values (i.e. cheating at golf) to dominate.

The Great Gatsby Chapters 8-9

Reading Activity 7: Meaning and Inferences

Anchor Standard	11th-12th Grade
CCRA.R.1	RL.11-12.1
CCRA.SL.1	SL.11-12.1

Objective

Students will answer questions about selected passages from the text which require them to extract meaning or inferences from the text.

Directions

The following pages contain passages from Chapters 8-9 of *The Great Gatsby* and questions related to the passages that require close reading to answer. Students should answer the questions related to the passages.

This can be done as a whole-class activity, individually, or in small groups. If it is done individually or in small groups, come together as a class to discuss the answers to the questions.

Follow-Up/Assessment/Extension

Collect the worksheets for review and/or grading. Ask students to keep these as possible raw material for writing essays in the future.

The Great Gatsby Chapters 8-9: Meaning & Inferences 1

Read the passages and answer the related questions.

1. He knew that Daisy was extraordinary, but he didn't realize just how extraordinary a "nice" girl could be. She vanished into her rich house, into her rich, full life, leaving Gatsby — nothing. He felt married to her, that was all.

What is the definition of marriage here?

2. "Wilson's glazed eyes turned out to the ashheaps, where small gray clouds took on fantastic shape and scurried here and there in the faint dawn wind."

What does this suggest about Wilson's state of mind?

3. "'Tom,' I inquired, 'what did you say to Wilson that afternoon?' He stared at me without a word, and I knew I had guessed right about those missing hours. I started to turn away, but he took a step after me and grabbed my arm."

What has Nick "guessed right about"? What is Tom's attitude about that?

4. "On the last night, with my trunk packed and my car sold to the grocer, I went over and looked at that huge incoherent failure of a house once more. On the white steps an obscene word, scrawled by some boy with a piece of brick, stood out clearly in the moonlight, and I erased it, drawing my shoe raspingly along the stone. Then I wandered down to the beach and sprawled out on the sand."

What is Nick trying to preserve here? Why?

5. "I couldn't forgive him or like him, but I saw that what he had done was, to him, entirely justified. It was all very careless and confused. They were careless people, Tom and Daisy — they smashed up things and creatures and then retreated back into their money or their vast carelessness, or whatever it was that kept them together, and let other people clean up the mess they had made. . . ."

What is the significance of the ellipses here?

The Great Gatsby Chapters 8-9: Meaning & Inferences 1 Suggested Answers

Read the passages and answer the related questions.

1. He knew that Daisy was extraordinary, but he didn't realize just how extraordinary a "nice" girl could be. She vanished into her rich house, into her rich, full life, leaving Gatsby — nothing. He felt married to her, that was all.

What is the definition of marriage here?
For Gatsby, his association with Daisy and her appeal to him is almost completely transactional. He wants what she represents ("rich house," "rich, full life") and when she "vanishes," he is left with "nothing." Marriage is a relationship which entitles Gatsby to Daisy as almost a dowry.

2. "Wilson's glazed eyes turned out to the ashheaps, where small gray clouds took on fantastic shape and scurried here and there in the faint dawn wind."

What does this suggest about Wilson's state of mind?
This passage suggests that Wilson is not completely in touch with reality, as if his imagination is taking over, filling in with thoughts of Myrtle's affair.

3. "'Tom,' I inquired, 'what did you say to Wilson that afternoon?' He stared at me without a word, and I knew I had guessed right about those missing hours. I started to turn away, but he took a step after me and grabbed my arm." What has Nick "guessed right about"? What is Tom's attitude about that?
Nick presumed correctly that Tom sent Wilson directly to Gatsby. Tom's action in the passage speaks volumes—he pursues Nick ("took a step") and then physically interacts with him ("grabbed my arm"). Tom's aggressive behavior suggests that he is right and fully justified, and he is forceful about conveying that to Nick.

4. "On the last night, with my trunk packed and my car sold to the grocer, I went over and looked at that huge incoherent failure of a house once more. On the white steps an obscene word, scrawled by some boy with a piece of brick, stood out clearly in the moonlight, and I erased it, drawing my shoe raspingly along the stone. Then I wandered down to the beach and sprawled out on the sand."

What is Nick trying to preserve here? Why?
The steps are white, part of a motif that connect Gatsby and Daisy to their past and his dream for the future. There is a purity to that that dream, and Nick erases the profane word to protect the purity of Gatsby's dream, even if it is implausible.

5. "I couldn't forgive him or like him, but I saw that what he had done was, to him, entirely justified. It was all very careless and confused. They were careless people, Tom and Daisy — they smashed up things and creatures and then retreated back into their money or their vast carelessness, or whatever it was that kept them together, and let other people clean up the mess they had made. . . ." What is the significance of the ellipses here?

Ellipses function as an omission, and it suggests that they never again take any responsibility in the death of Gatsby and that they will be party to more "careless" acts.

The Great Gatsby Chapters 8-9: Meaning & Inferences 2

Read the passage and answer the related questions.

"They're a rotten crowd," I shouted across the lawn. "You're worth the whole damn bunch put together."

I've always been glad I said that. It was the only compliment I ever gave him, because I disapproved of him from beginning to end. First he nodded politely, and then his face broke into that radiant and understanding smile, as if we'd been in ecstatic cahoots on that fact all the time. His gorgeous pink rag of a suit made a bright spot of color against the white steps, and I thought of the night when I first came to his ancestral home, three months before. The lawn and drive had been crowded with the faces of those who guessed at his corruption-and he had stood on those steps, concealing his incorruptible dream, as he waved them good-by.

I thanked him for his hospitality. We were always thanking him for that-I and the others.

"Good-by," I called. "I enjoyed breakfast, Gatsby."

1. How does this passage make Nick a hypocrite?

2. What do the words “crowd” and “bunch” signify?

3. What is the difference between Gatsby’s polite nod and “radiant and understanding smile”?

4. How do the words “corruption” and “incorruptible” work together in the passage?

5. What is the overall tone of the passage?

The Great Gatsby Chapters 8-9: Meaning & Inferences 2

Read the passage and answer the related questions.

"They're a rotten crowd," I shouted across the lawn. "You're worth the whole damn bunch put together."

I've always been glad I said that. It was the only compliment I ever gave him, because I disapproved of him from beginning to end. First he nodded politely, and then his face broke into that radiant and understanding smile, as if we'd been in ecstatic cahoots on that fact all the time. His gorgeous pink rag of a suit made a bright spot of color against the white steps, and I thought of the night when I first came to his ancestral home, three months before. The lawn and drive had been crowded with the faces of those who guessed at his corruption-and he had stood on those steps, concealing his incorruptible dream, as he waved them good-by.

I thanked him for his hospitality. We were always thanking him for that-I and the others.

"Good-by," I called. "I enjoyed breakfast, Gatsby."

1. How does this passage make Nick a hypocrite?
   Nick had formerly declared that he reserved judging people. Here he admits to "disapprov[ing]" of Gatsby. Also, his compliment ranks Gatsby above the others, as if Gatsby is a better, more moral or more valuable person.

2. What do the words "crowd" and "bunch" signify?
   Both are plural and general and suggest that Daisy, Tom, Jordan, et al., do not function as individuals but as members of a group ruled by its own immutable values and mores.

3. What is the difference between Gatsby's polite nod and "radiant and understanding smile"?
   The "polite nod" is the "Great Gatsby," the character that Jay Gatz plays. The "radiant and understanding smile" is the authentic person.

4. How do the words "corruption" and "incorruptible" work together in the passage?
   The use of the opposite words in the same sentence creates tension and causes the reader to reevaluate the primary way that Gatsby was perceived by others, as infamous, someone "who killed a man," a bootlegger, or any of the fantastic rumors. Yet, Gatsby was completely faithful and committed to his dream—the man may have been "corruptible" as a successful criminal, but his dream could not be marred.

5. What is the overall tone of the passage?
   We see Nick's conciliatory attitude toward Gatsby—it is as if they make their peace, and Nick foreshadows that it is the last time they will interact.

The Great Gatsby Chapters 8-9

Writing Activity 1: Is Nick a Reliable Narrator?

Anchor Standard	11th-12th Grade
CCRA.SL.1	SL.11-12.1, 1a-1d
CCRA.SL.3	SL. 11-12.4
CCRA.W.1	W. 11-12.2
CCRA.W.2	W. 11-12.4
CCRA.W.4	W. 11-12.5
CCRA.W.5	W. 11-12.7
	W. 11-12.9, 9b

Objectives

- Students will evaluate and analyze textual evidence to determine how the most dramatic chapter in the novel develops the theme of moral failure.
- Students will evaluate passages that show how characters engage in behavior that is not strictly moral.
- Students will examine language for biases and judgments.
- Students will write a composition in which they consider their analysis of relevant passages to answer the question, "How is moral failure significant in The Great Gatsby?"

Directions

The following series of worksheets and information organizers can be used by students individually, in small groups, or done partly as a whole-class activity. They are intended to guide students through the process of reading and thinking critically about information by ultimately answering the single question, "Is Nick a reliable Narrator?

Preview the following pages. Determine the best way to have your particular class handle this assignment (individually, pairs, groups, whole-class, or some combination). A combination of group work (to do the analyzing of the text on the chart page) followed by individual work (to do the second and third pages of the assignment) would most likely be best to fulfill the standards listed for this assignment.

Follow-Up/Assessment/Extension

- The written assignment will be a good basis for assessment of the students' success with this assignment. Create a rubric explaining the criteria on which their written assignments will be evaluated.
- Ask students to revisit the first few pages of the novel to review the "rules for living" that Nick describes and attempts to follow.
- Have some students read/present their writing assignments to the class to practice more speaking/listening skills and to expose all students to each others' ideas.
- Use this assignment to discuss the significance of a biased narrator and how that creates meaning in a work of literature.

The Great Gatsby Chapters 8-9: Is Nick A Reliable Narrator?

F. Scott Fitzgerald employs a relatively minor, ancillary character to convey the story of the title character through first-person narration. Information about Gatsby and his world is filtered through Nick, who claims to be both honest and non-judgmental. Through close reading of the text, determine whether Nick is a reliable narrator, and how your answer to that question affects the way meaning is perceived in the novel. How does Nick's role as narrator affect a larger understanding of the plot and characters? How does Nick's perspective shift the novel?

Using textual evidence from chapters 8-9, look for key moments in the narration to answer the question: Is Nick a reliable narrator?

To explore this question:

1. Identify passages and quotes which exemplify Nick in his role as narrator, particularly moments when he directly interrupts the text and draws attention to storytelling.

2. Examine the context of your quotes.

3. Consider the connotation and denotation of key phrases in your quotes.

    a. Are there judgmental words or phrases?
    b. What does Nick suggest about his role as narrator?
    c. Do Nick's observations fit with his moral code (honest, non-judgmental)?
    d. Is Nick explaining why or how he is telling Gatsby's story?

4. Review passages for patterns to determine what the significance of Nick's reliability as narrator is.

The Great Gatsby Chapter 8-9: Is Nick A Reliable Narrator?

Use this chart (and additional pages, if needed) to collect, analyze and evaluate information about Nick as narrator.

Observation from the text (quotes)	Paraphrase quote	Is the quote biased or judgmental in any way?	What does the quote suggest about Nick as a narrator?

The Great Gatsby Chapters 8-9

Suggested Writing Assignments

Anchor Standard	11th-12th Grade
CCRA.W.1	W.11-12.1, 1a-1e
CCRA W.2	W.11-12.2, 2a-2f
CCRA.W.3	W.11-12.3, 3a-3e
CCRA.W.4	W.11-12.4
CCRA.W.5	W. 11-12.5

Objective

Students will be assigned or will choose one of a selection of writing assignments pertaining to Chapters 8-9 of *The Great Gatsby* to fulfill one or more of the standards listed above.

Directions

To provide you with maximum flexibility for differentiated instruction, the following page has a list of suggested writing assignments, all related to Chapters 8-9 of *The Great Gatsby*. Either assign individual students particular assignments to do or allow students to choose their own assignments.

A second page of "Quick Write" topics is also included.

Follow-Up/Assessment/Extension

- Have dramatic readings of students' narratives or poems.
- Create a "reading room" space in your classroom where students can donate their writing assignments for others in the class to read.
- Allow students to do more than one assignment if they want to.
- Use the "left-over" assignments (not chosen for this activity) as topics for journal entries.

The Great Gatsby Chapters 8-9: Creative Analytical Writing Assignments

1. Write a newspaper report of the murder/suicide incident on Gatsby's property.

2. Write a eulogy for Gatsby by Nick.

3. Write a paragraph which expresses Daisy's thoughts when she learns that Gatsby has been murdered.

4. Write dialogue from Catherine that explains what she knew about her sister's life—make it true or use discretion.

5. Write a description of the West that urges people who moved East to return home.

6. Describe the trip that Tom and Daisy hastily take.

7. Imagine Gatsby had a will. What objects might he leave to Nick?

8. Write a book review of "Nick's book," with an awareness of the scandalous news of Gatsby and Wilson.

9. Why does Nick feel compelled to write a book about Gatsby? Write an epilogue to "Nick's book" that explains why.

10. Write a poem inspired by the last line of the novel: So we beat on, boats against the current, borne back ceaselessly into the past.

The Great Gatsby Chapters 8-9: Quick-Write Writing Assignments

1. Why is Nick unable to sleep at the beginning of Chapter 8? How does that connect with larger themes in the novel?
2. What does Nick's compliment to Gatsby suggest about Nick's propensity not to judge others?
3. What does Klipspringer represent?
4. How does Wilson view and understand T.J. Eckleburg? How does Michaelis respond?
5. Why does Nick become the spokesperson for Gatsby's estate? Why does he arrange the funeral?
6. What do Gatsby and his father have in common?
7. Is Wilson a mad man?
8. Is Gatsby's funeral similar to his parties? If so, how? If not, why not?
9. Was Nick's relationship with Jordan destined to fail? Why?
10. If Tom believes that Gatsby got what he deserved, by the same logic, did Myrtle or Tom get what they deserved?

MATERIALS: OVERVIEW

THE GREAT GATSBY

Reading Activity 1: True or False

Reading Activity 2: Analyzing Passages

Reading Activity 3: Character Culpability

Reading Activity 4: Action, Character, Decision

Reading Activity 5: Figurative Language

Reading Activity 6: Elements of Fiction & Literary Devices

Reading Activity 7: Meaning and Inferences

Writing Activity 1: Moral Failure In The Great Gatsby

Suggested Writing Assignments

Quick-Write Assignments

NOTES
THE GREAT GATSBY

The Great Gatsby Overview

Reading Activity 1: True or False?

Anchor Standard	11th-12th Grade
CCRA.R.1	RL.11-12.1
CCRA.SL1	SL.11-12.1
CCRA SL.4	SL.11-12.4

Objectives

- Students will be able to cite the parts of the text that support their analysis of what the text says or infers.
- Students will consider statements about the text, determine whether those statements are true or false, and will give textual evidence supporting their choices.
- Students will work together in small groups to discuss, analyze, and evaluate the statements made.
- Students will evaluate the analytical work of their peers.

Directions

Prior to completing novel: Give students (or post) the following list of statements about the chapters, and explain to students that they should read Overview to find out if these statements are true or false:

Daisy never loved Tom.
Daisy is directly responsible for Myrtle's death.
Nick notes that Gatsby's funeral was as well attended as his parties. Gatsby became interested in self-improvement only after meeting Dan Cody.
Daisy's hope for her daughter is that she grows up to be a fool.
Ultimately, Jordan believes that Nick is neither honest nor straightforward.

After reading Overview: The worksheets on the following pages can be done by students individually, in small groups, or as a whole class. Below are directions to use the questions as a group activity to fulfill more state standards:

- Cut the worksheet apart, making each question and answer box a slip.
- Divide your class into six groups and give one question and a True/False evaluation form to each group. Tell students they are to discuss the statement and determine if the statement is true or false, supporting their decision with evidence from the text. Tell them their answers will be evaluated on the criteria given on the evaluation form.
- Give students ample time to discuss the statements and record their answers.
- Have the groups swap True or False question slips so that each group can evaluate another group's answer. The group should fill in the number of the question they are evaluating, decide how well the answer fulfills the criteria listed, and fill out the form accordingly.
- Repeat the previous step until all the groups have evaluated each others' answers.
- Collect the evaluations and answer slips.

The Great Gatsby Overview: True or False?

Write *True* or *False* in the blank next to each statement. Below the statement, explain why you chose true or false, referencing the text to support your choices.

_________ 1. Daisy never loved Tom.

_________ 2. Daisy is directly responsible for Myrtle's death.

_________ 3. Nick notes that Gatsby's funeral was as well attended as his parties.

_________ 4. Gatsby became interested in self-improvement only after meeting Dan Cody.

_________ 5. Daisy's hope for her daughter is that she grows up to be a fool.

_________ 6. Ultimately, Jordan believes that Nick is neither honest nor straightforward.

The Great Gatsby Overview True or False? Evaluation

List Your Group's Members: Your Group's Question # _______

___________________ ___________________ ___________________

___________________ ___________________ ___________________

1 = No, Not At All **2** = A Little **3** = Some **4** = Yes **5** = Yes, Very Well

Evaluation of Question # ___

Does the explanation support the answer of true or false? 1 2 3 4 5
Is there good textual evidence to support the answer? 1 2 3 4 5
Is the answer clearly stated? 1 2 3 4 5
Total Score ________ of a possible 15 points

Evaluation of Question # ___

Does the explanation support the answer of true or false? 1 2 3 4 5
Is there good textual evidence to support the answer? 1 2 3 4 5
Is the answer clearly stated? 1 2 3 4 5
Total Score ________ of a possible 15 points

Evaluation of Question # ___

Does the explanation support the answer of true or false? 1 2 3 4 5
Is there good textual evidence to support the answer? 1 2 3 4 5
Is the answer clearly stated? 1 2 3 4 5
Total Score ________ of a possible 15 points

Evaluation of Question # ___

Does the explanation support the answer of true or false? 1 2 3 4 5
Is there good textual evidence to support the answer? 1 2 3 4 5
Is the answer clearly stated? 1 2 3 4 5
Total Score ________ of a possible 15 points

Evaluation of Question # ___

Does the explanation support the answer of true or false? 1 2 3 4 5
Is there good textual evidence to support the answer? 1 2 3 4 5
Is the answer clearly stated? 1 2 3 4 5
Total Score ________ of a possible 15 points

The Great Gatsby Overview: True or False? Suggested Answers

Write *True* or *False* in the blank next to each statement. Below the statement, explain why you chose true or false, referencing the text to support your choices.

<u>FALSE</u> 1. Daisy never loved Tom.

> Though this is what Gatsby is desperate for Daisy to claim, she cannot. After entreating her to admit in front of Tom that she never loved him, she does, but with "perceptible reluctance." Tom rejects her claim, because Daisy is lying.

<u>TRUE</u> 2. Daisy is directly responsible for Myrtle's death.

> Nick does not quite follow Gatsby's description of the accident, "and suddenly [he] guessed at the truth." He asks Gatsby, "Was Daisy driving?" Gatsby admits the truth—that Daisy was driving and struck Myrtle with the car, killing her.

<u>FALSE</u> 3. Nick notes that Gatsby's funeral was as well attended as his parties.

> Virtually no one attends Gatsby's funeral, and this disgusts Nick. Speaking with Owl Eyes, who makes an excuse for not coming to the house, Nick remarks that no one else came either. Owl Eyes exclaims: "Why, my God! They used to go there by the hundreds."

<u>FALSE</u> 4. Gatsby became interested in self-improvement only after meeting Dan Cody.

> While "the strange story of his youth with Dan Cody" is part of Jay Gatz's transformation into Jay Gatsby, Gatsby's father shows Nick a copy of a book that Gatsby had written in as a boy. The notes catalogue Gatsby's efforts at transforming himself into a successful man of character. His father also tells stories about Gatsby's aspiring to be different than his parents, who Gatsby criticized as being unrefined.

TRUE 5. Daisy's hope for her daughter is that she grows up to be a fool.

Learning that her baby was a girl, Daisy "turned [her] head away and wept." She says, "I hope she'll be a fool—that's the best thing a girl can be in this world, a beautiful little fool." This suggests that women cannot control their destinies because they are powerless compared to men, and must accept the poor choices of the men in their lives. To "be a fool" would be to be too ignorant to notice or care about men's indiscretions.

TRUE 6. Ultimately, Jordan believes that Nick is neither honest nor straightforward.

She recalls when he criticized her driving and warned her against meeting another "bad driver." She infers that Nick is a "bad driver": "I mean it was careless of me to make such a wrong guess. I thought you were rather an honest, straightforward person. I thought it was your secret pride." Ultimately she feels that Nick's ambivalence toward her is dishonesty.

The Great Gatsby Overview

Reading Activity 2: Analyzing Passages

Anchor Standard	11th-12th Grade
CCRA.R.6	RL.11-12.1
	RL.11-12.4
CCRA.SL.1	SL.11-12.1

Objectives

- Students will cite strong and thorough textual evidence to support analysis of what the text says explicitly as well as inferences drawn from the text, including determining where the text leaves matters uncertain.
- Students will determine the meaning of words and phrases as they are used in the text, including figurative and connotative meanings; analyze the impact of specific word choices on meaning and tone, including words with multiple meanings or language that is particularly fresh, engaging, or beautiful.
- Students will analyze a case in which grasping a point of view requires distinguishing what is directly stated in a text from what is really meant (e.g., satire, sarcasm, irony, or understatement).
- Students will analyze the impact of specific word choices on meaning and tone

Directions

On the pages that follow, there are 8 passages to analyze, each with a question or questions to guide the process. There are many ways to use these questions:

- You could use them as a worksheet for all students to complete individually.
- You could use the worksheet as your guide in a whole-class discussion. Have students turn to the first passage in the book, read it, and then ask the question(s) orally. Repeat through all 8 questions.
- You could assign one passage to each of 8 different groups of students, for the students to discuss and come up with responses to the question(s). Then hold a whole-class discussion.
- You could read the passage and then see which student can find the passage first (to practice skimming skills). Then follow up with the questions(s) and discussion.
- You could have students choose one or two questions to respond to in writing in their notebooks or journals.

Follow-Up/Assessment/Extension

- Ask students to gather passages that relate to the influences of Dan Cody on Gatsby.
- Have students write about the descriptions of the main characters who attend Gatsby's party, particularly Tom and Daisy.
- Have students pick out other passages in this chapters that show interesting word usage, descriptions, or lack of clarity.
- As an introduction to this activity, ask students to write about relationships, and whether or not affairs are ever justified. Ask students to examine characters' attitudes about this topic.

The Great Gatsby Overview Analyzing Passages

Answer the questions following the quotations completely.

1. "He had one of those rare smiles with a quality of eternal reassurance in it that you may come across four or five times in life. It faced, or seemed to face, the whole external world for an instant and then concentrated on you with an irresistible prejudice in your favor. It understood you just as far as you wanted to be understood, believed in you as you would like to believe in yourself."

   What does the quality of Gatsby's smile reflect about his own hopes?

2. "That's my Middle West — not the wheat or the prairies or the lost Swede towns, but the thrilling returning trains of my youth, and the street lamps and sleigh bells in the frosty dark and the shadows of holly wreaths thrown by lighted windows on the snow. I am part of that, a little solemn with the feel of those long winters, a little complacent from growing up in the Carraway house in a city where dwellings are still called through decades by a family's name. I see now that this has been a story of the West, after all — Tom and Gatsby, Daisy and Jordan and I, were all Westerners, and perhaps we possessed some deficiency in common which made us subtly unadaptable to Eastern life." What makes their story "a story of the West?"

   What does that mean?

3. "He was content to be alone--he stretched out his arms toward the dark water in a curious way, and as far as I was from him, I could have sworn he was trembling. Involuntarily I glanced seaward--and distinguished nothing except a single green light."

   Is Gatsby alone? Explain your answer.

4. "Almost five years! There must have been moments even that afternoon when Daisy tumbled short of his dreams--not through her own fault, but because of the colossal vitality of his illusion. It had gone beyond her, beyond everything. He had thrown himself into it with a creative passion, adding to it all the time, decking it out with every bright feather that drifted his way."

   What does the repetition of "beyond" suggest?

5. "But he didn't despise himself and it didn't turn out as he had imagined. He had intended, probably, to take what he could and go-but now he found that he had committed himself to the following of a grail. He knew that Daisy was extraordinary, but he didn't realize just how extraordinary a "nice" girl could be. She vanished into her rich house, into her rich, full life, leaving Gatsby-nothing. He felt married to her, that was all."

   What is significant about the tone of the last line?

6. "'She's got an indiscreet voice,' I remarked. 'It's full of ——' I hesitated.'
   'Her voice is full of money,' he said suddenly.
   That was it. I'd never understood before. It was full of money — that was the inexhaustible charm that rose and fell in it, the jingle of it, the cymbals' song of it. . . . high in a white palace the king's daughter, the golden girl. . ."

   What does this suggest about Daisy? About the way Gatsby views her?

7. "Some time toward midnight Tom Buchanan and Mrs. Wilson stood face to face discussing, in impassioned voices, whether Mrs. Wilson had any right to mention Daisy's name. 'Daisy! Daisy! Daisy!' shouted Mrs. Wilson. 'I'll say it whenever I want to! Daisy! Dai —'

   Making a short deft movement, Tom Buchanan broke her nose with his open hand."

   What is the significance of using full and formal names?

8. "'I spoke to her,' he muttered, after a long silence. 'I told her she might fool me but she couldn't fool God. I took her to the window.'— with an effort he got up and walked to the rear window and leaned with his face pressed against it ——'and I said 'God knows what you've been doing, everything you've been doing. You may fool me, but you can't fool God!''

   Standing behind him, Michaelis saw with a shock that he was looking at the eyes of Doctor T. J. Eckleburg, which had just emerged, pale and enormous, from the dissolving night.

   'God sees everything,' repeated Wilson.

   'That's an advertisement,' Michaelis assured him. Something made him turn away from the window and look back into the room. But Wilson stood there a long time, his face close to the window pane, nodding into the twilight."

   What is significant about T.J. Eckleburg being an advertisement?

The Great Gatsby Overview Analyzing Passages

Answer the questions following the quotations completely.

1. "He had one of those rare smiles with a quality of eternal reassurance in it that you may come across four or five times in life. It faced, or seemed to face, the whole external world for an instant and then concentrated on you with an irresistible prejudice in your favor. It understood you just as far as you wanted to be understood, believed in you as you would like to believe in yourself."

   What does the quality of Gatsby's smile reflect about his own hopes?
   Gatsby's smile provides exactly what he himself seeks: to be taken at face value, or to be fully accepted as the face he shows the world. The power of his smile is about the ability to validate another person's identity (and even their most idealized identity).

2. "That's my Middle West — not the wheat or the prairies or the lost Swede towns, but the thrilling returning trains of my youth, and the street lamps and sleigh bells in the frosty dark and the shadows of holly wreaths thrown by lighted windows on the snow. I am part of that, a little solemn with the feel of those long winters, a little complacent from growing up in the Carraway house in a city where dwellings are still called through decades by a family's name. I see now that this has been a story of the West, after all — Tom and Gatsby, Daisy and Jordan and I, were all Westerners, and perhaps we possessed some deficiency in common which made us subtly unadaptable to Eastern life."

   What makes their story "a story of the West?" What does that mean?
   They brought with them to the East their habits, practices, beliefs and predilections. The West, as Nick describes it, is the permanent home, the place to return to during school break. The West has a social stratum which one's place in it is determined by one's last name and family lineage. Ultimately, they impressed these values on the East, which created ways for them to justify careless, harmful behavior.

3. "He was content to be alone--he stretched out his arms toward the dark water in a curious way, and as far as I was from him, I could have sworn he was trembling. Involuntarily I glanced seaward--and distinguished nothing except a single green light." Is Gatsby alone?
   Nick is wrong here, which highlights him as an unreliable narrator. Gatsby is embracing Daisy, at least the "incarnation" of her that he believes that he will fully possess one day.

4. "Almost five years! There must have been moments even that afternoon when Daisy tumbled short of his dreams--not through her own fault, but because of the colossal vitality of his illusion. It had gone beyond her, beyond everything. He had thrown himself into it with a creative passion, adding to it all the time, decking it out with every bright feather that drifted his way."

   What does the repetition of "beyond" suggest?
   The repetition emphasizes how far "beyond" Gatsby's machinations to reunite with Daisy have gone. The use of general words like "her" and "everything" in proximity to the repetition suggests that it isn't even Daisy herself that Gatsby so desires, but rather the generic archetype that she represents, a rich girl.

5. "But he didn't despise himself and it didn't turn out as he had imagined. He had intended, probably, to take what he could and go-but now he found that he had committed himself to the following of a grail. He knew that Daisy was extraordinary, but he didn't realize just how extraordinary a "nice" girl could be. She vanished into her rich house, into her rich, full life, leaving Gatsby-nothing. He felt married to her, that was all."

   What is significant about the tone of the last line?
   It is neither loving nor romantic, but more transactional. Marriage here seems to be a function of Gatsby's own materialistic desires. The repetition of the word "extraordinary" shows how he holds her—values her—in high esteem; the other repetition in the passage ("rich") echoes back to "extraordinary." Why was she "extraordinary"...because she was "rich."

6. "'She's got an indiscreet voice,' I remarked. 'It's full of ——' I hesitated.'
   'Her voice is full of money,' he said suddenly.
   That was it. I'd never understood before. It was full of money — that was the inexhaustible charm that rose and fell in it, the jingle of it, the cymbals' song of it. . . . high in a white palace the king's daughter, the golden girl. . ."

   What does this suggest about Daisy? About the way Gatsby views her?
   To have a voice "full of money" suggests that Daisy has some intrinsic value about her. To have a voice "full of money" is both empowering and disempowering. To have a voice that is valued is a way to command attention.

7. "Some time toward midnight Tom Buchanan and Mrs. Wilson stood face to face discussing, in impassioned voices, whether Mrs. Wilson had any right to mention Daisy's name. 'Daisy! Daisy! Daisy!' shouted Mrs. Wilson. 'I'll say it whenever I want to! Daisy! Dai —'

   Making a short deft movement, Tom Buchanan broke her nose with his open hand."

   What is the significance of using full and formal names?
   The use of formal names for Tom and Myrtle ("Mrs. Wilson") highlights their extramarital affair—they are not married and do not share the same last name. Interestingly, Daisy's name is informal here, suggesting she is less important.

8. "'I spoke to her,' he muttered, after a long silence. 'I told her she might fool me but she couldn't fool God. I took her to the window.'— with an effort he got up and walked to the rear window and leaned with his face pressed against it ——'and I said 'God knows what you've been doing, everything you've been doing. You may fool me, but you can't fool God!''

   Standing behind him, Michaelis saw with a shock that he was looking at the eyes of Doctor T. J. Eckleburg, which had just emerged, pale and enormous, from the dissolving night.

   'God sees everything,' repeated Wilson.

   'That's an advertisement,' Michaelis assured him. Something made him turn away from the window and look back into the room. But Wilson stood there a long time, his face close to the window pane, nodding into the twilight."

   What is significant about T.J. Eckleburg being an advertisement?
   Michaelis's comment is important and grave—he recognizes that Wilson is not thinking clearly. The highlighting of the word "advertisement" connects directly back to the hotel scene when Daisy tells Gatsby that he looks like an advertisement. It is exactly then when Tom has a moment of realization about the nature of Gatsby and Daisy's relationship. So, what does it mean to "be" an advertisement? It means to convey a concept or idea more than a truth. From this, the reader can extrapolate that Fitzgerald is not making a larger statement about religion in the context of behavior and morality. Just as Wilson does not belong to a church, he is wrong and deluded on this point.

The Great Gatsby Overview

Reading Activity 3: Character Culpability

Anchor Standard	11th-12th Grade
CCRA.R.1	RL.11-12.1
CCRA.SL.1	SL.11-12.1

Objective

Using textual evidence, students will explore how characters are responsible for conflict.

Directions

The character culpability worksheet on the following page could be used in many ways, completed by small groups of students, individual students, or as a whole class activity.

Students will be able to identify which characters create the main conflicts in the novel. Students can revisit this assignment later in the unit to further investigate which characters changed and in what ways.

After students complete the worksheets discuss students' answers as a whole class. Collect the worksheets for grading, if you choose, or have students put them in their notebooks for further study.

Follow-Up/Assessment/Extension

Revisit this assignment later in the unit and discuss how the characters are culpable in small groups or as a whole class.

The Great Gatsby Overview Reading Activity 3: Character Culpability

Sometimes in literature, the heroes and villains of a story are clear. In this novel, morally ambiguous behavior makes determining the characters' culpability for the downfall of others more complicated.

Consider the ultimate outcomes for Gatsby and Myrtle. Which characters are most culpable for these outcomes?

Rank the main characters on a continuum based on textual evidence of how culpable they are for the tragic outcomes. Jot down reasons to justify your rankings.

Jordan | Nick | Gatsby | Daisy | Tom | Myrtle | Wilson

LEAST CULPABLE

Name	Reason For Ranking In This Place

MOST CULPABLE

The Great Gatsby Overview
Reading Activity 3: Character Culpability Suggested Answers

Sometimes in literature, the heroes and villains of a story are clear. In this novel, morally ambiguous behavior makes determining the characters' culpability for the downfall of others more complicated.

Consider the ultimate outcomes for Gatsby and Myrtle. Which characters are most culpable for these outcomes?

Rank the main characters on a continuum based on textual evidence of how culpable they are for the tragic outcomes. Jot down reasons to justify your rankings.

Jordan | Nick | Gatsby | Daisy | Tom | Myrtle | Wilson

Answers will vary. As long as the reasons are valid, almost any order is acceptable. Here's one opinion:

Jordan: She helps reunite Daisy and Gatsby and is present during the confrontation between Gatsby and Tom, but does not contribute directly in other ways to the tragic outcome.

Nick: He helps reunite Daisy and Gatsby, and has socialized with Tom and Myrtle. He tries to counsel Gatsby to let go of the past.

Gatsby: He orchestrates his life to reunite with Daisy, knowing she is married. He participates in an extramarital affair. He is willing to take responsibility for the accident.

Myrtle: She participates in an extramarital affair and causes an accident by attempting to confront Tom and running into the street.

Daisy: She participates in an extramarital affair and drives the car that kills Myrtle. She allows Gatsby to take blame for accident.

Wilson: He does not participate in an extramarital affair, but in response to learning that his wife has, he plans to murder the person he believes is her lover. He commits suicide after murdering Gatsby. Wilson is the only character who mentions God's awareness of immoral behavior.

Tom: He engages in extramarital affairs regularly. He "scornfully" directs Daisy to ride back to Long Island with Gatsby, and then implies Gatsby's guilt for Myrtle's death.

The Great Gatsby Overview
Reading Activity 4: Action, Character, Decision

Anchor Standard	11th-12th Grade
CCRA.R.1	RL.11-12.1
CCRA.SL.1	SL.11-12.1

Objective
Students will identify particular lines of dialogue or incidents in the story that propel the action, reveal aspects of character, or provoke a decision.

Directions
The following page contains passages from the Overview of *The Great Gatsby*. Students should determine whether the passages advance the action, reveal aspects of a character, or provoke a decision.

This can be done as a whole-class activity, individually, or in small groups.

Follow-Up/Assessment/Extension
Have students skim the Overview in the text to find one example of a passage that propels the action, one that reveals aspects of a character, and one that provokes a decision. Again, this could be done individually or as a group. This activity can be a quick prompt for starting class discussion of a reading assignment.

The Great Gatsby Overview: Action, Character, Decision

Write **A** (for Action) **C** (for Character) or **D** (for Decision) in the blank next to each to identify whether the passage/statement advances the action, tells us more about a character, or provokes a decision. On the lines under each question, provide a short explanation of your choice.

___ 1. On the other hand, no garage man who had seen him ever came forward, and perhaps he had an easier, surer way of finding out what he wanted to know.

___ 2. "And Daisy ought to have something in her life," murmured Jordan to me.

___ 3. Two shining arrogant eyes had established dominance over his face and gave him the appearance of always leaning aggressively forward. Not even the effeminate swank of his riding clothes could hide the enormous power of that body — he seemed to fill those glistening boots until he strained the top lacing, and you could see a great pack of muscle shifting when his shoulder moved under his thin coat. It was a body capable of enormous leverage — a cruel body.

___ 4. I think it was on the third day that a telegram signed Henry C. Gatz arrived from a town in Minnesota. It said only that the sender was leaving immediately and to postpone the funeral until he came.

___ 5. "Jimmy was bound to get ahead. He always had some resolves like this or something. Do you notice what he's got about improving his mind? He was always great for that. He told me I et like a hog once, and I beat him for it."

___ 6. "Miss Baker?" he inquired. "I beg your pardon, but Mr. Gatsby would like to speak to you alone."

The Great Gatsby Overview:

Action, Character, Decision Suggested Answers

Write **A** (for Action) **C** (for Character) or **D** (for Decision) in the blank next to each to identify whether the passage/statement advances the action, tells us more about a character, or provokes a decision. On the lines under each question, provide a short explanation of your choice.

A 1. On the other hand, no garage man who had seen him ever came forward, and perhaps he had an easier, surer way of finding out what he wanted to know.
The passage describes Wilson's inquiry into who owned the yellow car; the passage intimates that Tom tells him ("easier" and "surer"). This discovery moves the plot and dramatic ending of the novel forward.

D 2. "And Daisy ought to have something in her life," murmured Jordan to me.
Jordan makes the decision to reunite Daisy and Gatsby, setting aside any moral qualms about it based on the fact that she is aware that Tom is unfaithful to Daisy.

C 3. Two shining arrogant eyes had established dominance over his face and gave him the appearance of always leaning aggressively forward. Not even the effeminate swank of his riding clothes could hide the enormous power of that body — he seemed to fill those glistening boots until he strained the top lacing, and you could see a great pack of muscle shifting when his shoulder moved under his thin coat. It was a body capable of enormous leverage — a cruel body.
Tom's personality is illuminated by the description of his body, which is ultimately "cruel." Tom represents a hyper-masculine archetype, corporeal, aggressive, territorial, and party to multiple extramarital affairs.

A 4. I think it was on the third day that a telegram signed Henry C. Gatz arrived from a town in Minnesota. It said only that the sender was leaving immediately and to postpone the funeral until he came.
The unexpected announcement and arrival of Gatsby's father serves to move the action forward, highlighting the pathetic dichotomy that was Gatsby—highly "successful," but beloved and remembered by very few.

C 5. "Jimmy was bound to get ahead. He always had some resolves like this or something. Do you notice what he's got about improving his mind? He was always great for that. He told me I et like a hog once, and I beat him for it."
Gatsby's father perfectly illuminates Gatsby's proclivity toward self-improvement from even a very young age. Gatsby was never content with his station in life or identity, and constantly sought means for improving them to become the person he believed that he actually was.

A 6. "Miss Baker?" he inquired. "I beg your pardon, but Mr. Gatsby would like to speak to you alone."
This simple request sets in motion all the action of the book, from facilitating Daisy's reunion with Gatsby to the fallout of the recklessness of the parties involved.

The Great Gatsby Overview

Reading Activity 5: Figurative Language

Anchor Standard	11th-12th Grade
CCRA.R.4	RL.11-12.4
CCRA.SL.1	SL.11-12.1

Objectives

- Students will determine the meaning of words and phrases as they are used in the text, including figurative and connotative meanings.
- Students will determine whether passages from the text are examples of simile, metaphor or idiom.

Directions

The following page has passages from the text which exemplify simile, metaphor or idiom. This work-sheet can be done individually, as a whole-class activity, or in small groups. Discuss the answers as a whole class. Collect the worksheets and record the grades if you choose to do so.

Follow-Up/Assessment/Extension

Ask students to notice which characters use these types of figurative language. Is it primarily the narrator? Specific characters? What is the effect of this on the reader?

The Great Gatsby Overview: Figurative Language

On the short line provided, write **S** for simile, M for metaphor or **I** for idiom. On the lines under each question, explain the meaning and specifically how the figurative language helps create meaning.

___ 1. "She took it into the tub with her and squeezed it up into a wet ball, and only let me leave it in the soap-dish when she saw that it was coming to pieces like snow."

___ 2. "I've got my hands full."

___ 3. "This is a valley of ashes — a fantastic farm where ashes grow like wheat into ridges and hills and grotesque gardens; where ashes take the forms of houses and chimneys and rising smoke and, finally, with a transcendent effort, of men who move dimly and already crumbling through the powdery air."

___ 4. "This is a valley of ashes — a fantastic farm where ashes grow like wheat into ridges and hills and grotesque gardens; where ashes take the forms of houses and chimneys and rising smoke and, finally, with a transcendent effort, of men who move dimly and already crumbling through the powdery air."

___ 5. "The only completely stationary object in the room was an enormous couch on which two young women were buoyed up as though upon an anchored balloon."

The Great Gatsby Overview: Figurative Language Suggested Answers

On the short line provided, write **S** for simile, M for metaphor or **I** for idiom. On the lines under each question, explain the meaning and specifically how the figurative language helps create meaning.

S 1. "She took it into the tub with her and squeezed it up into a wet ball, and only let me leave it in the soap-dish when she saw that it was coming to pieces like snow."
The comparison of the pieces to snow uses "like," and is therefore a simile. The imagery created suggests that the letter was so damaged—and by extension that Daisy is so distraught—that the letter has become tiny and fragmented.

I 2. "I've got my hands full."
Unsurprisingly, Nick offers an idiom to Gatsby in response to his offer for sideline work what is not completely legal. By using an idiom, Nick can convey his meaning indirectly, without having to refuse Gatsby directly.

M 3. "<u>This is a valley of ashes — a fantastic farm</u> where ashes grow like wheat into ridges and hills and grotesque gardens; where ashes take the forms of houses and chimneys and rising smoke and, finally, with a transcendent effort, of men who move dimly and already crumbling through the powdery air."
The area near Wilson's garage is directly compared to a valley or farm, which is ironic since those suggest vibrant, fertile, green spaces, but this "valley" is lifeless and bereft.

S 4. "This is a valley of ashes — a fantastic farm where <u>ashes grow like wheat</u> into ridges and hills and grotesque gardens; where ashes take the forms of houses and chimneys and rising smoke and, finally, with a transcendent effort, of men who move dimly and already crumbling through the powdery air."
The comparison of the ashes to the wheat uses "like" and is therefore a simile. The landscape is barren and grey, but the comparison to wheat suggests the Midwest, alluding to the thematic tension between East and West which plays out in the narrative.

S 5. "The only completely stationary object in the room was an enormous couch on which two young women were buoyed up as though upon an anchored balloon."
The position of Daisy and Jordan on the couch ("buoyed") is directly compared to an "anchored balloon," and is therefore a simile. The comparison evokes the nautical/boating motif that pervades the novel.

The Great Gatsby Overview

Reading Activity 6: Elements of Fiction & Literary Devices

Anchor Standard	11th-12th Grade
CCRA.R.1	RL.11-12.1
	RL.11-12.2
	RL.11-12.4
	RL.11-12.5
CCRA.SL.1	SL.11-12.1

Objective
Students will study and discuss passages from the text to examine symbol, motif and theme and explore how these create meaning in the text.

Directions
Use the following discussion questions as a guide to discussing symbol, motif and theme, in these chapters. You can give students the questions ahead of time and have them formulate answers prior to the class discussion or you can jump right in with a whole class discussion without student preparation if your students will handle that well.

As you hold the class discussion, be sure to include conversations defining symbol, motif and theme and explaining how these work together to advance meaning in the text.

Follow-Up/Assessment/Extension
After your discussion, ask students to look for recurrences of these symbols, motifs and themes in future chapters.

The Great Gatsby Overview: Elements of Fiction & Literary Devices

1. Throughout the book, the theme of being "self-made" plays a large role. In what ways does this theme show up throughout Gatsby's actions?

2. Refer to the passage below:

> "She's got an indiscreet voice," I remarked. "It's full of——" I hesitated.
>
> "Her voice is full of money," he said suddenly.
>
> That was it. I'd never understood before. It was full of money—that was the inexhaustible charm that rose and fell in it, the jingle of it, the cymbals' song of it. . . . high in a white palace the king's daughter, the golden girl. . . (120)

This passage depicts a couple of different themes that are portrayed throughout the book. Select one and connect this passage to another moment in the novel.

3. Consumerism and materialism are themes in the novel. How do Gatsby's material possessions reflect his moral values? Refer to at least 2 different individual items owned by Gatsby/Gatz that are mentioned in the novel.

4. Refer to the passage below:

> The "death car." as the newspapers called it, didn't stop; it came out of the gathering darkness, wavered tragically for a moment, and then disappeared around the next bend. (137)

Relate the above passage to Gatsby's life.

5. What does the green light symbolize?

6. One of the novel's motifs is sports. Consider the role this motif plays in the novel and its significance.

The Great Gatsby Overview: Elements of Fiction & Literary Devices ANSWER KEY

1. Throughout the book, the theme of being "self-made" plays a large role. In what ways does this theme show up throughout Gatsby's actions?

Gatsby literally invents himself ("Jay Gatsby sprang from his Platonic conception of himself"), creating a lifestyle that he felt was more befitting to who he really was. One example is the copy of *Hopalong Cassidy* which his father shows Nick. In it he creates a list of ways to develop discipline and mastery over himself as well as a schedule for committing to these practices for improving his life and bettering himself. Another example is Gatsby's house, which has been decked out "with every bright feather that drifted his way." Gatsby's rise through Wolfsheim's ranks into a highly successful bootlegger is another—albeit less legitimate—way that Gatsby has "made" himself. Finally, Gatsby's clothes and affect (such as his use of "Old Sport" as a familiar address) are more superficial ways that he has "self-made" his public persona.

2. Refer to the passage below:

> "She's got an indiscreet voice," I remarked. "It's full of——" I hesitated.
>
> "Her voice is full of money," he said suddenly.
>
> That was it. I'd never understood before. It was full of money—that was the inexhaustible charm that rose and fell in it, the jingle of it, the cymbals' song of it. . . . high in a white palace the king's daughter, the golden girl. . . (120)

This passage depicts a couple of different themes that are portrayed throughout the book. Select one and connect this passage to another moment in the novel.

Multiple themes—love/attraction, consumerism, and class—all resonate in this famous quote. Her voice is not only "indiscreet," meaning that it does not take pains to be modest and that it attracts attention, but it is "full of money." Nick repeats Gatsby's reply, which further emphasizes the point. Daisy is then an object, and an object of value, but one—like money—determined not intrinsically, but by the value set by the market. These concepts underscore how Daisy is objectified by both Gatsby and Tom.

3. Consumerism and materialism are themes in the novel. How do Gatsby's material possessions reflect his moral values? Refer to at least 2 different individual items owned by Gatsby/Gatz that are mentioned in the novel.

Gatsby is about conspicuous consumption—his silk shirts, his hydroplane, his yellow car, his house, his pink suit. All of these are ostentatious and showy possessions of someone with wealth who lacks social class. Gatsby's possessions from before he became wealthy—his little boat and his *Hopalong Cassidy* book suggest that he has always been aspirational and in pursuit of material things.

4. Refer to the passage below:

> The "death car." as the newspapers called it, didn't stop; it came out of the gathering darkness, wavered tragically for a moment, and then disappeared around the next bend. (137)

Relate the above passage to Gatsby's life.

This passage echoes an unkind sentiment about Gatsby said by Tom, that people just do not show up out of nowhere and obtain a house like Gatsby's. The incident is described like Gatsby himself—showing up suddenly out of nowhere, being involved in a tragedy and disappearing. Gatsby, though notorious, had virtually no one show up to mourn him—"disappearing" into obscurity. The passage also unites Gatsby and Myrtle as similar tragic figures.

5. What does the green light symbolize?

The light serves as a physical manifestation of Gatsby's desire for Daisy. His desire is not for love or sentimentality or even physical lust, but for her as an "incarnation" as the ultimate material prize for living a "successful" life. While Gatsby's dream to reunite with Daisy may seem romantic, it is an impossibility, at least in the way Gatsby has designed to literally attempt to recreate the past.

6. One of the novel's motifs is sports. Consider the role this motif plays in the novel and its significance.

Tom is associated with sports, as a formidable former college football player, and is even introduced around Gatsby's party as a polo player, which Tom dislikes. To introduce him in that way is a deliberate slight on Gatsby's part as it relegates Tom from the world of business to the world of leisure—he's not a businessman, but a player. Jordan is a professional athlete, and it is often invoked in physical descriptions. She is not unfeminine, per se, but she is described differently than Daisy, and sports moderates that difference. Jordan is also associated with cheating during sports (connecting her to Tom, in a way, through the dual meaning of "cheating"). Finally Meyer Wolfsheim is noted for fixing the World's Series—again an example of cheating and individual will. As Nick points out, he never conceived of a single individual making a decision that had such far-reaching consequences.

The Great Gatsby Overview

Reading Activity 7: Meaning and Inferences

Anchor Standard	11th-12th Grade
CCRA.R.1	RL.11-12.1
CCRA.SL.1	SL.11-12.1

Objective

Students will answer questions about selected passages from the text which require them to extract meaning or inferences from the text.

Directions

The following pages contain passages from Overview of *The Great Gatsby* and questions related to the passages that require close reading to answer. Students should answer the questions related to the passages.

This can be done as a whole-class activity, individually, or in small groups. If it is done individually or in small groups, come together as a class to discuss the answers to the questions.

Follow-Up/Assessment/Extension

Collect the worksheets for review and/or grading. Ask students to keep these as possible raw material for writing essays in the future.

The Great Gatsby Overview: Meaning & Inferences 1

Read the passages and answer the related questions.

1. Refer to the passage below:

> "Meyer Wolfshiem? No, he's a gambler." Gatsby hesitated, then added coolly: "He's the man who fixed the World's Series back in 1919."
>
> "Fixed the World's Series?" I repeated.
>
> The idea staggered me. I remembered, of course, that the World's Series had been fixed in 1919, but if I had thought of it at all I would have thought of it as a thing that merely HAPPENED, the end of some inevitable chain. It never occurred to me that one man could start to play with the faith of fifty million people—with the single-mindedness of a burglar blowing a safe.
>
> "How did he happen to do that?" I asked after a minute.
>
> "He just saw the opportunity."

What does this passage reveal about Nick's characterization?

2. Refer to the passage below:

> In my younger and more vulnerable years my father gave me some advice that I've been turning over in my mind ever since.
>
> "Whenever you feel like criticizing any one," he told me, "just remember that all the people in this world haven't had the advantages that you've had."

Does Nick follow this advice or not? Why is this significant?

3. Refer to the passage below:

> The other car, the one going toward New York, came to rest a hundred yards beyond, and its driver hurried back to where Myrtle Wilson, her life violently extinguished, knelt in the road and mingled her thick dark blood with the dust. (137)

Respond to the quote above, focusing specifically on one of the words underlined above.

4. Refer to the passage below:

> His parents were shiftless and unsuccessful farm people—his imagination had never really accepted them as his parents at all. The truth was that Jay Gatsby of West Egg, Long Island, sprang from his Platonic conception of himself. He was a son of God—a phrase which, if it means anything, means just that—and he must be about His Father's business, the service of a vast, vulgar, and meretricious beauty. So he invented just the sort of Jay Gatsby that a seventeen-year-old boy would be likely to invent, and to this conception he was faithful to the end. (98)

How does this passage represent Gatsby's belief in changing oneself (and one's past) in order to change one's destiny?

5. Refer to the passage below:

> But he knew that he was in Daisy's house by a colossal accident. However glorious might be his future as Jay Gatsby, he was at present a penniless young man without a past, and at any moment the invisible cloak of his uniform might slip from his shoulders. So he made the most of his time. He took what he could get, ravenously and unscrupulously— eventually he took Daisy one still October night, took her because he had no real right to touch her hand.
>
> He might have despised himself, for he had certainly taken her under false pretenses. I don't mean that he had traded on his phantom millions, but he had deliberately given Daisy a sense of security; he let her believe that he was a person from much the same stratum as herself—that he was fully able to take care of her. As a matter of fact, he had no such facilities—he had no comfortable family standing behind him, and he was liable at the whim of an impersonal government to be blown anywhere about the world.

Does Gatsby feel the need to take Daisy as a possession? Explain what this reveals about Gatsby <u>or</u> Daisy.

The Great Gatsby Overview: Meaning & Inferences 1 Suggested Answers

Read the passages and answer the related questions.

1. Refer to the passage below:

> "Meyer Wolfsheim? No, he's a gambler." Gatsby hesitated, then added coolly: "He's the man who fixed the World's Series back in 1919."
>
> "Fixed the World's Series?" I repeated.
>
> The idea staggered me. I remembered, of course, that the World's Series had been fixed in 1919, but if I had thought of it at all I would have thought of it as a thing that merely HAPPENED, the end of some inevitable chain. It never occurred to me that one man could start to play with the faith of fifty million people—with the single-mindedness of a burglar blowing a safe.
>
> "How did he happen to do that?" I asked after a minute.
>
> "He just saw the opportunity."

What does this passage reveal about Nick's characterization?

Nick is a relatively naïve, moral person. He is not a self-centered person. The word "staggered" suggests that Nick is genuinely taken aback by the thought of "one man" affecting "fifty million people." The "single-mindedness" that Wolfsheim exhibits is not unlike how Gatsby relates to Daisy. Both of these ideas—manipulating the world for one's own gain—is practically foreign to Nick.

2. Refer to the passage below:

> In my younger and more vulnerable years my father gave me some advice that I've been turning over in my mind ever since.
>
> "Whenever you feel like criticizing any one," he told me, "just remember that all the people in this world haven't had the advantages that you've had."

Does Nick follow this advice or not? Why is this significant?

Ultimately, no, Nick does not follow this advice fully during the course of the novel. He criticizes and judges others, particularly Tom and Daisy, though they have more than he does, plus the same or better "advantages." Nick criticizes Wolfsheim's pathetic excuses for not attending Gatsby's funeral as well as Kilpspringer, following his request for his forgotten athletic shoes. At points in the novel, Nick does criticize Gatsby ("…you can't recreate the past…"), but obliges to Gatsby's ways.

3. Refer to the passage below:

> The other car, the one going toward New York, came to rest a hundred yards beyond, and its driver hurried back to where Myrtle Wilson, her life violently extinguished, knelt in the road and mingled her thick dark blood with the dust. (137)

Respond to the quote above, focusing specifically on one of the words underlined above.

The garage is literally between Long Island and New York, making it a traversed path used by reckless people like Daisy, Tom and Gatsby. New York is the location for business and organized crime, a metropolis that produces the ashes that litter this area. It is a playground for the wealthy, as the group rented space at the exclusive Plaza Hotel just to have drinks.

The use of Myrtle's last name is deliberate. It signifies that she is married, and it creates a layer of formality between the narrator/Nick and Myrtle, as if they are not on a "first-name basis." The party in her apartment in Chapter 2 similarly uses her last name. The juxtaposition of her married name and the phrase "her life," is evocative, because as "Myrtle Wilson," she did not lead the kind of life that she wanted to lead, intimating that she was fooled by her husband into believing that he was more established and that they would have a better life than they had.

4. Refer to the passage below:

> His parents were shiftless and unsuccessful farm people—his imagination had never really accepted them as his parents at all. The truth was that Jay Gatsby of West Egg, Long Island, sprang from his Platonic conception of himself. He was a son of God—a phrase which, if it means anything, means just that—and he must be about His Father's business, the service of a vast, vulgar, and meretricious beauty. So he invented just the sort of Jay Gatsby that a seventeen-year-old boy would be likely to invent, and to this conception he was faithful to the end. (98)

How does this passage represent Gatsby's belief in changing oneself (and one's past) in order to change one's destiny?

Gatsby seems to believe that the power of belief in an individual can override the natural laws of the universe. He does not accept his parents; he finds a surrogate father in Dan Cody. He gives birth to a fiction, "a conception," (called Jay Gatsby) and believes it, which, to him, makes it truth.

5. Refer to the passage below:

But he knew that he was in Daisy's house by a colossal accident. However glorious might be his future as Jay Gatsby, he was at present a penniless young man without a past, and at any moment the invisible cloak of his uniform might slip from his shoulders. So he made the most of his time. He took what he could get, ravenously and unscrupulously— eventually he took Daisy one still October night, took her because he had no real right to touch her hand.

He might have despised himself, for he had certainly taken her under false pretenses. I don't mean that he had traded on his phantom millions, but he had deliberately given Daisy a sense of security; he let her believe that he was a person from much the same stratum as herself—that he was fully able to take care of her. As a matter of fact, he had no such facilities—he had no comfortable family standing behind him, and he was liable at the whim of an impersonal government to be blown anywhere about the world.

How is love commoditized here?

Gatsby did not have means ("penniless") to be a suitable potential suitor for Daisy, so he "took" her under false pretenses. "Penniless" Gatsby has "no real right to touch her hand," which would require being of the "same stratum." Money would give Gatsby access. In the absence of money, he exploits his position in the military (which stratifies its soldiers regardless of income) to gain entry into her world. The description "ravenously and unscrupulously" can be applied to how Gatsby eventually gains his wealth, the wealth which almost gave him access to winning back Daisy.

The Great Gatsby Overview: Meaning & Inferences 2

Read the passage and answer the related questions.

On the last night, with my trunk packed and my car sold to the grocer, I went over and looked at that huge incoherent failure of a house once more. On the white steps an obscene word, scrawled by some boy with a piece of brick, stood out clearly in the moonlight, and I erased it, drawing my shoe raspingly along the stone. Then I wandered down to the beach and sprawled out on the sand.

Most of the big shore places were closed now and there were hardly any lights except the shadowy, moving glow of a ferryboat across the Sound. And as the moon rose higher the inessential houses began to melt away until gradually I became aware of the old island here that flowered once for Dutch sailors' eyes — a fresh, green breast of the new world. Its vanished trees, the trees that had made way for Gatsby's house, had once pandered in whispers to the last and greatest of all human dreams; for a transitory enchanted moment man must have held his breath in the presence of this continent, compelled into an aesthetic contemplation he neither understood nor desired, face to face for the last time in history with something commensurate to his capacity for wonder.

And as I sat there brooding on the old, unknown world, I thought of Gatsby's wonder when he first picked out the green light at the end of Daisy's dock. He had come a long way to this blue lawn, and his dream must have seemed so close that he could hardly fail to grasp it. He did not know that it was already behind him, somewhere back in that vast obscurity beyond the city, where the dark fields of the republic rolled on under the night.
Gatsby believed in the green light, the orgastic future that year by year recedes before us. It eluded us then, but that's no matter — to-morrow we will run faster, stretch out our arms farther. . . . And one fine morning ——

So we beat on, boats against the current, borne back ceaselessly into the past.

1. Why is the beach a significant setting?

2. What are "the last and greatest of all human dreams"?

3. How is Gatsby's "wonder" different than the explorers' "wonder"?

4. What does the green light symbolize?

5. What is the significance of how the final sentence of the second to last paragraph is punctuated?

The Great Gatsby Overview: Meaning & Inferences 2 Suggested Answers

Read the passage and answer the related questions.

On the last night, with my trunk packed and my car sold to the grocer, I went over and looked at that huge incoherent failure of a house once more. On the white steps an obscene word, scrawled by some boy with a piece of brick, stood out clearly in the moonlight, and I erased it, drawing my shoe raspingly along the stone. Then I wandered down to the beach and sprawled out on the sand.

Most of the big shore places were closed now and there were hardly any lights except the shadowy, moving glow of a ferryboat across the Sound. And as the moon rose higher the inessential houses began to melt away until gradually I became aware of the old island here that flowered once for Dutch sailors' eyes — a fresh, green breast of the new world. Its vanished trees, the trees that had made way for Gatsby's house, had once pandered in whispers to the last and greatest of all human dreams; for a transitory enchanted moment man must have held his breath in the presence of this continent, compelled into an aesthetic contemplation he neither understood nor desired, face to face for the last time in history with something commensurate to his capacity for wonder.

And as I sat there brooding on the old, unknown world, I thought of Gatsby's wonder when he first picked out the green light at the end of Daisy's dock. He had come a long way to this blue lawn, and his dream must have seemed so close that he could hardly fail to grasp it. He did not know that it was already behind him, somewhere back in that vast obscurity beyond the city, where the dark fields of the republic rolled on under the night.
Gatsby believed in the green light, the orgastic future that year by year recedes before us. It eluded us then, but that's no matter — to-morrow we will run faster, stretch out our arms farther. . . . And one fine morning ——

So we beat on, boats against the current, borne back ceaselessly into the past.

1. Why is the beach a significant setting?
The novel has a nautical/boat motif that is strongly connected to Gatsby. He changes his identity and fortune in a boat, then works on a boat for Dan Cody where he becomes more sophisticated, and he dies floating on a pool raft. The beach is also associated with summer, and Nick has been encouraged by Gatsby to use his beach. Nick being on the beach associates him with the motif, and with Gatsby, for whom he has a remarkable sense of empathy.

2. What are "the last and greatest of all human dreams"?
It is to be the first to find something valuable and have it to yourself—here, discoverers on a voyage finding New York.

3. How is Gatsby's "wonder" different than the explorers' "wonder"?
Gatsby believed that he could be the sole possessor of the thing he wanted—Daisy. He could not, as her love for Tom could not be undone or erased.

4. What does the green light symbolize?
The light is the intense dream that Gatsby believed in and hoped to accomplish (remaking the present to resemble and feel like the past, when Gatsby and Daisy were in love in Louisville), but it was inevitably going to fail, as he confused the future with the past.

5. What is the significance of how the final sentence of the second to last paragraph is punctuated?
The punctuation includes two dashes which signify interruption. The first dash is like Gatsby making a declaration to believe at any cost, which is followed by Fitzgerald's characteristic ellipses which signal an omission (and in the novel, several ellipses passages are romantic encounters) the hopeful phrase "And one fine morning," which is then interrupted suddenly, similar to the murder of Gatsby by Wilson and the sudden death of his dream.

The Great Gatsby Overview

Writing Activity 1: How Is The Great Gatsby A Tragedy, And What's To Be Learned From It?

Anchor Standard	11th-12th Grade
CCRA.SL.1	SL.11-12.1, 1a-1d
CCRA.SL.3	SL. 11-12.4
CCRA.W.1	W. 11-12.2
CCRA.W.2	W. 11-12.4
CCRA.W.4	W. 11-12.5
CCRA.W.5	W. 11-12.7
	W. 11-12.9

Objectives

- Students will research to find the elements of a tragedy.
- Students will evaluate, analyze, and synthesize textual evidence to determine whether or not The Great Gatsby fits the definition of a "tragedy."
- Students will write a composition in which they consider their analysis of relevant passages and textual information to answer the question, "How is *The Great Gatsby* a tragedy, and what is to be learned from it?"

Directions

The following series of worksheets and information organizers can be used by students individually, in small groups, or done partly as a whole-class activity. They are intended to guide students through the process of reading and thinking critically about information by ultimately answering the question, "How is The Great Gatsby a tragedy, and what is to be learned from it?"

Preview the following pages. Determine the best way to have your particular class handle this assignment (individually, pairs, groups, whole-class, or some combination). A combination of group work (to do the analyzing of the text on the chart page) followed by individual work (to do the second and third pages of the assignment) would most likely be best to fulfill the standards listed for this assignment.

Follow-Up/Assessment/Extension

- The written assignment will be a good basis for assessment of the students' success with this assignment. Create a rubric explaining the criteria on which their written assignments will be evaluated.
- Have some students read/present their writing assignments to the class to practice more speaking/listening skills and to expose all students to each others' ideas.
- Have students compare the tragic elements in The Great Gatsby to elements in another tragic work they have studied.
- Let students act out some of the most dramatic tragic scenes from The Great Gatsby.

The Great Gatsby Overview:
How Is The Great Gatsby A Tragedy And What's To Be Learned From It?

A "tragedy" can be defined as a literary work in which the "hero" or some great person suffers defeat or destruction caused by a flaw in character or some overriding power, such as fate or societal forces.

Consider that definition as it may apply to The Great Gatsby.

- Who is the "hero" who suffers defeat or destruction? Is there more than one?
- What causes that destruction? (There could be multiple causes.)
    - Character flaw(s)?
    - Involvement with others?
    - Others' character flaws?
    - Societal forces?
    - Fate?

After you determine the cause of the hero's destruction, think about the story as a whole and determine what lessons we can learn from it.

Part I:
Which character(s) suffer defeat and/or destruction in The Great Gatsby? State the character's name, how that character was destroyed or defeated, and the page number in the text where that destruction is evidenced.

Character	What Happened?	Page Ref.

Part II

Use this chart (and additional pages, if needed) to collect, analyze and evaluate information. Put your line items from the What Happened column on the chart on the previous page in the What Happened column below. Working left to right, trace back the causes of the events to their roots.

What Happened? →	Immediate Cause →	What Caused The Immediate Cause? →	What Caused That? What Is The Root Cause, The Root of the Problem?

Part III

Look at the Root Causes column on the chart you completed on the previous page. Review the kinds of things that are there. They could be things like greed, pride, desires for social standing, selfishness, loneliness, or many others.

Consider these things and the effects they have had on the characters in the book. Look at how the characters have interacted with each other. Think about these things in context of the themes and other elements you have discussed in class, then come up with a list of things readers could/should learn from reading The Great Gatsby. Next to each item on your list, write a few sentences explaining what elements in the book brought you to that conclusion. Continue on additional pages if necessary.

Things To Be Learned From The Great *Gatsby*	**Elements In The Book That Support This Conclusion**

Extra Page For Notes or Additional Information from Part I, II, or III

The Great Gatsby Overview
Suggested Writing Assignments

Anchor Standard	11th-12th Grade
CCRA.W.1	W.11-12.1, 1a-1e
CCRA W.2	W.11-12.2, 2a-2f
CCRA.W.3	W.11-12.3, 3a-3e
CCRA.W.4	W.11-12.4
CCRA.W.5	W. 11-12.5

Objective
Students will be assigned or will choose one of a selection of writing assignments pertaining to Overview of *The Great Gatsby* to fulfill one or more of the standards listed above.

Directions
To provide you with maximum flexibility for differentiated instruction, the following page has a list of suggested writing assignments, all related to Overview of *The Great Gatsby*. Either assign individual students particular assignments to do or allow students to choose their own assignments.

A second page of "Quick Write" topics is also included.

Follow-Up/Assessment/Extension
- Have dramatic readings of students' narratives or poems.
- Create a "reading room" space in your classroom where students can donate their writing assignments for others in the class to read.
- Allow students to do more than one assignment if they want to.
- Use the "left-over" assignments (not chosen for this activity) as topics for journal entries.

The Great Gatsby Overview: Creative Analytical Writing Assignments

1. Imagine Gatsby wrote a plan for his life. Write a paragraph describing his plans to throw parties that would attract Daisy.

2. Write a poem about living in the Valley of Ashes.

3. Write dialogue between Jordan and Daisy in the "present" of the novel in which Jordan asks Daisy about what happened the night before her wedding.

4. Write a magazine article that interviews Jordan Baker about being a modern woman and female athlete.

5. Write a letter from Nick to Gatsby's father that explains the enclosed book he wrote about Gatsby.

6. Rewrite the first page of the novel as a prologue, revisiting the issues and advice that Nick raises. Reflect Nick's life experiences and new perspectives in the prologue.

7. Imagine Nick writes an autobiography. Create an outline of the major events.

8. Nick imagines that the decade of his thirties stretching ahead of him will be lonely. Write an account of what you believe happens to him.

9. Select an omitted scene that is represented by ellipses in the novel. Write a version of the scene.

10. Imagine that T.J. Eckleburg is an omniscient presence. Describe what T.J. Eckleburg has witnessed.

The Great Gatsby Overview: Quick-Write Writing Assignments

1. In the 1920s, cars were beginning to have a major effect on American society for the first time. What does the car symbolize in the novel?

2. Which woman is more progressive, Daisy or Jordan? Why?

3. Nick and Gatsby are both veterans of World War I. The war was the first war with wide scale modern technologies and large, multiple fronts. The devastation caused by the war was beyond that which had ever happened previously. How does this character detail affect their relationship and make them different than other characters?

4. Which character is the most careless? Why?

5. Is Nick a reliable narrator? Explain.

6. How does Fitzgerald's use of ellipses/omissions affect the narrative?

7. Nick conveys information about Gatsby in chapter 6 out of the sequence that he receives it. Why is this significant? How does this relate to Nick's father's advice at the very beginning of the novel?

8. The novel is set during Prohibition, so all drinking of alcohol would be illegal. Why do people like Tom, Nick and Gatsby's party guests break the law?

9. Why does Nick feel compelled to tell Gatsby's story?

10. What is the significance of making Gatsby a criminal? Does it affect characters' sympathy for him?

www.ingramcontent.com/pod-product-compliance
Lightning Source LLC
Chambersburg PA
CBHW081441070526
44586CB00019B/2197
* 9 7 8 1 6 0 2 4 9 5 0 2 9 *